ADVA...
Your ...

"The picture-obsessed, highly edited, perfection-driven culture we live in makes most of us feel like we never quite measure up. I'm so thankful for Chelsea's young-but-strong voice calling girls to understand God's bigger plan and purpose as you discover your own beautiful."

—LYSA TERKEURST, *NEW YORK TIMES* BESTSELLING
AUTHOR AND PRESIDENT OF PROVERBS 31 MINISTRIES

"Whether it's a YouTube video or her debut book, it's obvious to see that Chelsea's greatest desire is to lead others to Christ. I'm so excited to see where Chelsea's journey takes her next—I know it will be beautiful!"

—JAMIE GRACE, AWARD-WINNING MUSICIAN AND SPEAKER

"*Your Own Beautiful* is full of advice and tips, but the chief reason this book is helpful is that it speaks primarily to Scripture's definition of beauty. I'm proud of Chelsea, and the way she models Jesus-centered identity to millions of young people."

—LOUIE GIGLIO, PASTOR OF PASSION CITY CHURCH, FOUNDER OF PASSION
CONFERENCES, AND AUTHOR OF *GOLIATH MUST FALL*

"Within minutes of first meeting Chelsea, I couldn't help but notice the beautiful person she is. Her smile. Her kindness. Everyone in the room was drawn to her. What was it? You could see the beauty of God within her. In these pages and through Chelsea's words, you'll begin to see the beauty of God inside you. I pray you'll see a glimpse of just how beautiful you are."

—ADAM WEBER, PASTOR OF EMBRACE CHURCH
AND AUTHOR OF *TALKING WITH GOD*

"I'm a big fan of Chelsea Crockett. For years she has impacted millions of viewers with her joy-filled personality and charm, and now God is using her to tell a story bigger than her own. Her new book takes you along on her adventurous journey, giving plenty of helpful advice along the way, and helping you see what true beauty looks like."

—Matt Brown (@evangelistmatt), evangelist, author, and founder of Think Eternity

ADVICE &
INSPIRATION
FROM
CHELSEA
CROCKETT

YOUR
OWN
Beautiful

ZONDERVAN®

ZONDERVAN

Your Own Beautiful
Copyright © 2017 by Beauty Licious, Inc.

This title is also available as a Zondervan ebook.

Requests for information should be addressed to:
Zondervan, *3900 Sparks Dr. SE, Grand Rapids, Michigan 49546*

ISBN 978-0-310-76236-2

17 18 19 20 21 22 23 24 25 /DSC/ 20 19 18 17 16 15 14 13 12 11 10 9 8 7 6 5 4 3 2 1

CONTENTS

FOREWORD

What makes me beautiful?

If you're like me, you may have asked yourself this question, oh . . . a million times. Through television, magazine covers, and in movies, the world offers lots of different answers to that question. Some answers may say that you need to dress a certain way or have a certain type of body. As women, we can feel a lot of pressure to live by these standards and conform to the world's definition of beauty.

A few years ago, when I was blessed with the opportunity to be on *Dancing with the Stars*, I realized that there's a battle going on in the hearts and minds of young women. The world and the Bible show two completely different ways to live, and each leads to a very different outcome. The truth is that God tells us how to live because he wants us to experience his joy and live beautiful, extraordinary lives.

I like to encourage young women to live original by making different choices than others around them. Every day, we're confronted with false messages about our bodies, our worth, and our purpose. Choosing to live in a way God says is best takes a lot of courage, but it also comes with big rewards.

When I first saw Chelsea's YouTube videos, I could tell she was someone who was beautiful inside and out. As we began getting to know each other, I was impressed with how she boldly lived her faith. Her joy was truly contagious. (She also totally saved me with her tech-savvy skills when I was trying to upload a video to YouTube!) I see a huge need for a book like *Your Own Beautiful*—one that gives awesome beauty advice while helping young women discover who God has made them to be. The practical tips in this book will help you look and feel beautiful from the inside out as you build strong relationships, overcome peer pressure, and develop a deeper relationship with God.

I am so excited that you have this chance to meet my friend Chelsea, whose warmth, honesty, and humor will win your heart. I have a feeling you won't be able to put this book down once you start reading. And I pray that as you read it, you will find your own beautiful and live it out to the fullest.

Love,

Sadie Robertson

INTRODUCTION

I didn't set out to live my teenage years in front of a million people, but that's what happened.

A million people saw me get my braces off. A million people watched me tackle my first day of high school. A million people even saw me go on my first date.

Back when YouTube was mostly cute animal videos, budding young singers, and silly Annoying Orange videos, I used my desktop computer to record and upload my first beauty tutorial and start my YouTube channel, BeautyLiciousInsider.

The summer of 2011 was especially hot, and like most thirteen-year-olds living in Troy, Illinois (pop. 10,100), I was bored. I'd recently become obsessed with makeup and online beauty tutorials, so I decided to make my own video. Within a few months of uploading my first tutorial—how to create a gymnastics hairstyle—I was getting as many as 15,000 views on my videos, which covered everything from putting together a cute outfit to my morning routine to creating the perfect makeup for prom. Less than a year after I started my YouTube channel, I had 20,000 subscribers. Five years later, I had over 1.5 million.

The opportunities that have come my way through my YouTube channel have been amazing. I've been a finalist in the NYX Face Awards, appeared on national TV, had my own reality TV show, and met some incredible people. While it's a little weird to have all of your "firsts" documented online, it's also a big privilege. I've had the chance to reach millions of teens and help them face the tough things we all go through. (That's why I eventually expanded my YouTube offerings to include advice on life and faith.)

I don't know why you picked up this book. Maybe you're a fan of BeautyLiciousInsider (Hi!) and want to know more about how it started. Or maybe you just want some killer beauty and style tips to look and feel your best. Inside these pages, you'll find quick, simple ideas to look beautiful for school, a date night, a day at the beach, or when you're just hanging out and watching the big game with friends. Whether you want to create a stunning look for a special event or a sophisticated one for a job interview, I'll help you learn how to put it together. I'll even show you ways to hone your everyday look to let your natural beauty shine through.

I used to be pretty obsessed with trying to create the next big celebrity look or putting together the perfect outfit. I cared a lot about what others thought of me and whether or not they accepted me. But just like a great sports car has a beautiful exterior *and* a powerful engine, I needed to take a deeper look at what made me run. I discovered that although it felt good to look beautiful and be admired (and felt bad to be criticized or rejected), ultimately those things didn't bring true satisfaction or make me any happier. They also didn't help me when I was

going through something difficult, like dealing with friend drama, stress at school, or feeling rejected by a guy I liked.

Putting on makeup and choosing the perfect outfit *is* a lot of fun. But in the end, clothes and beauty products are not what make you feel beautiful. During my time on YouTube, I've learned a lot about what it means to let your beauty come from the inside out, and I want to share that with you.

There are many books out there about inner beauty and learning to love yourself, and confidence and self-esteem are really important. But I've discovered there's a lot more to life than liking what I see in the mirror and believing in myself. Each skill, each opportunity, each friend, and each moment is a gift from God. It took me awhile to really get this, but I finally see that he has big plans for me! He wants to use everything in my life—every joy, every struggle, even every mistake—for my good and his glory.

Inside this book, you'll read lots of behind-the-scenes details about my life and how BeautyLiciousInsider started, but I also want to share what I've learned since uploading that first video: that looking beautiful on the outside is great, but it will never satisfy your deepest longings to be accepted and valued. Only God, who created you and says you are priceless, can do that.

When I really let that truth sink in, I realized that even through challenges and trials in my life, God was creating beauty. Instead of life being all about me, it became about something bigger. Even though I hadn't always recognized God's presence in my life, he has been guiding me all along. He has put people in my life who encourage me and continually point me toward him. And the more I release my grip on my own plans, the more I discover what it truly means to be beautiful, and reflect his beauty to others.

As you read this book, I want you to know that you are more beautiful and valuable than you can possibly know. God has made you exactly the way you are for a reason. He loves you deeply, accepts you fully, and has a purpose for your life. It may not involve applying makeup (or going on your first date!) in front of a million people on YouTube, but you have your own stage—your friends, family, and those you influence every day. Wherever you are and whatever you're doing, you can display your own individual beauty as you reflect the most beautiful one of all.

XOXO,

Chels

CHAPTER 1

ALL ABOUT ME

Happy girls are the prettiest girls.

—AUDREY HEPBURN

I stood on the stage, clutching my new friend's hand. We had been called forward from a group of six finalists and soon would find out who would be the winner of the NYX Face Awards, which came with a $25,000 cash prize and a year's supply of NYX cosmetics. As the judges looked on and cameras flashed, celebrity gossip columnist Perez Hilton read the results.

I waited there with my stomach in my throat, thoughts swirling through my head. A year earlier I'd been a regular thirteen-year-old, living in a small Illinois town, playing basketball with my younger brother and his friends, and cutting the hair off my little sister's Barbies (just to mess with her and give them some individual style). I did normal middle school stuff, like going to class, hanging out with my family, and shopping at the mall with my friends.

Then I discovered makeup. It happened the summer before eighth grade, while I was still binge-watching Annoying Orange and Fred Figglehorn videos (also created by a thirteen-year-old). When a Michelle Phan video popped up as a suggestion, I watched my first makeup tutorial. I was hooked! I loved her techniques and was fascinated by the fact you could put something on your face and look totally different.

I began experimenting with the looks I saw online. I'd wear rainbow eye shadow or blue lipstick. I even played around with colored contacts.

That summer I was super bored, so I decided to try making my own beauty tutorial—a how-to on creating a gymnastics hairstyle—because I

BEST AND WORST VIDEOS

TOP 5 BEST VIDEOS

1. **Weirdest Swap EVER with RclBeauty101!** When Rachel Levin (RclBeauty101!) and I swapped our Black Friday finds, I ended up with a banana costume, a rainbow projector, and a Shar-Pei throw blanket. And you should see what I got her!

2. **Barbie Makeup Tutorial** My all-time most popular video features a tutorial my parents and I did together. Mom helped me find all of the pink accessories and set them up, and Dad filmed me giving myself a Barbie-inspired look. So pink!

3. **Chelsea after Wisdom Teeth Removal** Everyone dreads getting their wisdom teeth out, and you've probably seen the videos of people professing their love for a celebrity or thinking they're in the middle of a zombie apocalypse afterward. My reaction didn't disappoint.

4. **Vampire Makeup Tutorial** I had a blast making this Halloween vampire tutorial. It was so much fun to run around the woods and play with the editing to get that spook factor.

5. **My Brother Does My Makeup** Before my brother hit puberty, he had a super-squeaky, adorable voice, and I had him do my makeup. The result was, well, interesting. In another video, my sister and I returned the favor!

was taking gymnastics at the time. I used my Mac desktop computer to record the video and uploaded it to my YouTube channel, BeautyLicious-Insider. (When I picked the name, I knew I wanted my channel to be about beauty, and the "licious" came from my favorite lip gloss.)

I had no idea what I was doing at first. I used my webcam to record myself creating different hairstyles, makeup looks, and outfits. Then I used a microphone to create a voice-over, explaining how I created the look and the products I used. I edited the videos myself, adding music and effects.

TOP 5 WORST VIDEOS

1. **Gymnastics Hairstyle!** The very first video uploaded to my channel. Contrary to what I say, this hairstyle DOES NOT stay up for gymnastics, which is why I laugh every time I watch it. (My apologies to gymnasts everywhere!)

2. **My Everyday School Makeup, Hair, and Outfit!** This video looked legit, but in it I committed dozens of beauty crimes, including not blending my eye shadow, clumping my mascara, and wearing a shirt as a miniskirt! My subscribers were probably shocked, but there's a surprise at the end.

3. **Outfits for Winter!!** This was one of my first "fashion" videos. It was totally freezing during this entire shoot, and you see me shivering throughout! Plus, my friend Jordan and I positioned the camera in one spot and did a bunch of silly antics on a rock wall. Let's just say the videography leaves something to be desired.

4. **Spring Makeup!** I went to the back of my neighborhood to film this makeup tutorial. I applied makeup without a mirror, because I didn't know how to film a makeup tutorial on my own yet.

5. **Middle School Makeup Tutorial** I sat on the floor of my bathroom to apply minimal makeup to my eyes. Why? I then offer this little (now embarrassing) gem of advice: "The first step is you always want to wash your hands, but you don't really need to see me doing that. 'Cause, yeah."

I didn't expect anyone would watch my videos, but they did! After about a month, I was getting 5,000 to 15,000 views per video. At that time, I was one of the only thirteen-year-olds doing beauty tutorials on YouTube, and I think that's what drew other teens to my channel. I wanted my videos to feel like I was talking to friends, giving them advice on how to curl hair, do makeup for homecoming, or get ready for school in the morning. My goal was to make my viewers smile and help them feel beautiful, even though I definitely wasn't a YouTube pro back then.

I didn't know it that summer, but my big break was just around the corner.

BIG THINGS AHEAD

People who knew me growing up may have been surprised that I chose to represent myself as a beauty expert on YouTube. After all, until I was in middle school I was happy to wear basketball shorts most days and join my brother, Chandler, and his friends for a pick-up game of basketball or football. In those days, my younger sister, Kylie, was more of the girlie-girl, and I was the tomboy. I even tried to convince my parents to let me get a motocross bike at one point. (They said no.)

In Troy, Illinois, the small town where I've lived most of my life, there aren't a lot of reasons to look fancy. The only day of the week that I really remember dressing up was on Sunday. My family and I would put on our best outfits for church, and then go out to our favorite fried chicken restaurant for lunch.

My mom also dressed us up for the first day of school and made a huge deal about it. She would pack us special lunches and take our pictures as we got onto the bus. My mom, who is an elementary school reading specialist, has always had a flare for making things beautiful, so maybe that's where I first got my eye for fashion.

My childhood was *so* normal it was kind of a shock when my YouTube channel began to grow as fast as it did. Six months after it launched, I had about 15,000 subscribers. That's when I received an

email telling me about the NYX Face Awards—a competition sponsored by NYX Cosmetics to name the best beauty vlogger of the year.

I submitted my first video entry—"Spring Party Look"—to the competition in March 2012. I also upgraded from my webcam to a Canon digital video camera around that time so I could start making higher-quality videos. Once I made it into the top thirty, a huge box of NYX cosmetics showed up at my house to help me create my looks for the contest.

Every stage of the competition was so exciting, but it seemed impossible for me to make it into the top six. At fourteen, I was the youngest person in the contest, and I was competing against established beauty vloggers with twenty times the number of subscribers I had.

As a result, I just decided to have fun with it and see what happened.

After my spring party look, I submitted three 80s-inspired looks, a vampire look, and a fairy princess fantasy look. After I posted a video, I would tell all my friends at school to vote for me online. I kept my class updated on how I was doing, and soon almost the entire student body was voting for me! I kept getting enough votes to make it through to the next round.

Each time I made it to the next stage of competition, I received another box of goodies from NYX. Then I received the call that I had made it into the top six and would be flown to Los Angeles to tour the NYX headquarters and compete in the finals! I was so excited that I had to go outside and take a run to release some of my excess energy. I took my camera with me and made an emotional video, thanking my amazing fans for their support!

When I got to LA, I was put up in a fancy hotel, and I got to meet fellow competitor Charis (CharismaStarTV), who I'd only known through her videos. (She later became one of my best friends.) We visited the NYX headquarters, which was a makeup junkie's dream come true: the walls were lined with makeup, nail polish, and other beauty items. While touring NYX, we found out that the theme of our challenge would be "runway."

On the day of the competition, I had two hours to create an original makeup look for an African American model before she walked the runway in front of a panel of judges. I was so nervous! I had never done makeup on a model before, and I didn't have any experience working with darker skin tones since I'd only been creating looks on myself. But I did my best and went with an 80s-glam smoky eye.

After the runway show, as I stood on the stage, surrounded by some of the biggest names and influences in beauty, I had no idea what the results would be. One by one, Perez Hilton awarded four of the six finalists individual awards that acknowledged their specific strengths. Then he asked Charis and me to step forward.

As we stood there hand in hand, I felt the butterflies having a major dance party in my stomach. One of us was about to be named beauty vlogger of the year! Seconds seemed like minutes. Finally, Perez awarded me first runner-up and winner of the "Illuminative Award." Charis was the winner! I gave her a massive hug. I was so happy for my friend (who is beautiful inside and out) and humbled at being part of an amazing experience.

BEAUTYLICIOUS GROWTH

My success in the NYX Face Awards was what my YouTube channel needed to really take off. After the competition, my name was out there and new opportunities began pouring in. A lot of companies suddenly wanted me to promote their brands or work with them.

My subscriber base spiked from 20,000 to more than 100,000. To keep my new fans, I started aiming for more consistency by posting two to three videos per week and ramping up my presence on Facebook, Twitter, and Instagram.

Another great development for my channel was that my dad really came alongside me. During the competition, he was impressed by my dedication and could see the potential in what I was doing. So he started helping me, taking on the role of my manager and handling the business side of things, along with the filming.

Over time, we got multiple cameras and light sets and turned our basement into a studio for YouTube stuff. As the channel has grown, it's been cool to work with my dad and see him find his passion for videography and photography. My mom has also jumped in to help. When I filmed a Barbie makeup tutorial, Mom and I went shopping for all kinds of girlie, pink accessories, and she helped me arrange them in the filming area. That video is one of my favorites, and it went on to receive over 17 million views!

BEAUTYLICIOUSINSIDER TIMELINE

BeautyLiciousInsider has experienced some incredible moments. Here are some of the highlights:

July 3, 2011: Joined YouTube as BeautyLiciousInsider.

August 4, 2011: Uploaded my first video, "Gymnastics Hairstyle" on YouTube.

March 21, 2012: Entered the NYX Face Awards with my video submission "Spring Party Look."

May 13, 2012: Got my braces off. My parents took me into the orthodontist on a Saturday, where I learned they were surprising me with getting my braces off early!

May 28, 2012: Found out that I made it into the top six for the NYX Face Awards.

June 2, 2012: Uploaded "Barbie Makeup Tutorial," which went on to hit over 17 million views.

June 26, 2012: Flew to Los Angeles for the finals of the NYX Face Awards, where I toured the NYX headquarters and won first runner-up and the "Illuminative Award."

July 1, 2012: My family and I took a vacation to San Diego. Part of the video I made of the trip made it into a TV commercial!

February 7, 2013: Hit 150,000 subscribers.

November 25, 2013: Started marketing BeautyLicious merchandise, including T-shirts, hoodies, sunglasses, and sweatpants.

As I took a closer look at the YouTube beauty and lifestyle universe, I noticed that one technique people used to increase their subscribers was to collaborate with other YouTubers, filming videos together and then linking to each other's channels. This allowed them to share subscribers and make more connections than they could on their own. I wanted to put my own spin on some of the "collabs" I'd seen, so I came up with "swaps."

July 24, 2014: Appeared in my own show on the *Seventeen* channel called *#17Before17*, where I took viewers along through a seventeen-item bucket list of things I wanted to do before I turned seventeen.

September 15, 2014: Named a *Seventeen* magazine influencer.

February 2, 2015: Hit 1 million subscribers!

March 4, 2015: Appeared on *Morning Express with Robin Meade* on HNL.

March 23, 2015: My family was featured in the reality TV show *Beautylicious: Offline* on the HLNtv network.

May 12, 2015: Participated in giving dresses away to high school girls for prom through the Cinderella Project.

January 19, 2016: Uploaded a video of me sharing my Christian testimony.

May 2, 2016: Went to my senior prom.

May 26, 2016: Graduated from Triad High School.

July 26, 2016: Got a book deal!

August 20, 2016: Appeared on *TODAY* with Lysa TerKeurst, where we talked about Lysa's book *Uninvited* and overcoming rejection at any age.

August 26, 2016: Embarked on an epic 2,600-mile road trip with my dad to get to California Baptist University for college!

October 26, 2016: *Wish for Christmas* movie premiered.

January 2–4, 2017: Attended Passion Conference with over 50,000 college-age students in Atlanta, Georgia.

A fellow YouTuber and I would send each other a box full of random goodies and then make videos of ourselves opening the boxes and pulling out all the loot. Each swap had a theme, such as "USA vs. Canada," where my Canadian friend, Adelaine, sent me a box of Canadian goodies and I sent her a box of American stuff. I did a back-to-school swap, an

Illinois vs. California swap, a birthday swap, and even a Black Friday swap (with RclBeauty101, which turned out to be the funniest and most random swap ever!).

But even more fun than meeting other YouTubers was getting to know the people who were watching my videos. I didn't realize how much I would love meeting my subscribers. When you meet someone and she tells you that your video encouraged her or made her laugh or helped her learn something new, it's really special. It was inspiring to start making those personal connections with my fans, rather than just reading their comments online.

MORE THAN JUST A PRETTY FACE

When I first started my channel, I hadn't expected anyone to watch my videos. I would see a comment and think, "Oh, that's cool." Over time, however, each video ended up with thousands of comments, something I never would have expected. And as I read through them—some complimentary, others not so much—I started realizing that these were real people going through very real struggles, many of which I'd gone through myself.

This realization became clearer at the start of ninth grade. Just as my YouTube channel was really gaining traction, I attended a Christian event with some girls from my church. We stayed up half of the night talking about all the drama and struggles and pain we were going through. And though we were all experiencing different things, we realized each of us needed the Lord. That weekend, God showed me that I needed to hand over my life to him.

That decision to let God take over also had a larger effect. Whenever I saw the struggles my fans were going through, I now felt a strong desire to help them with more than their makeup—I wanted to offer people the same hope and help I was finding through my faith.

At that point I had just entered high school, and I saw firsthand that drama—whether it centered around boys, friends, family, school, or social events—was everywhere. Everyone I knew—myself included—had tons of screw-ups, worries, and flaws we were trying to hide from the world. So I started giving my subscribers a candid look into my personal life in videos I called "My Secret Diary!" and "Chelsea Lately."

In those videos, I didn't make my life look all shiny and perfect. The videos included confessions about feeling distant from my family, struggling in my walk with Christ, and not having friends at school. I shared my insecurities and heartaches, hoping that my honesty might help someone who was going through the same thing. I even asked my viewers to give me advice in the comments section.

I still did the beauty tutorials because they were fun, but made sure to sprinkle in videos with advice about relationships, faith, friendships, peer pressure, and family. While the advice videos didn't always get as many views as the beauty ones, I noticed from the comments section that a lot of people genuinely appreciated them. And it was rewarding to see that the content I was producing was really impacting people's lives. I knew that the deeper videos were what I was meant to do.

HOW DID I GET HERE . . . AND WHY?

By the time I turned seventeen, I marveled at what BeautyLiciousInsider had become. I had a million and a half subscribers from all over the world. I'd participated in brand deals with multiple Fortune 500 companies, appeared on billboards, and been featured in *Seventeen*, *Teen Vogue*, and *Shutter*. I'd recorded my own online TV show, *#17Before17*, on the *Seventeen* online channel, and been featured in a short-lived reality TV show about my family. Millions of young women looked to me for beauty and fashion advice, but also for guidance on how to live their lives. It was incredibly humbling, and it also felt like a big responsibility. I took my work seriously while still being my fun-loving self. I wanted to be an example to those who were watching.

At one event, a subscriber came up to me and began to cry, telling me how much my testimony about following Jesus had meant to her. That was a turning point for me; I realized that God had allowed my YouTube channel to flourish. I loved what I was doing, but there was nothing special about me. Not really. I was a pretty normal teen girl who happened to be good at makeup and not afraid to talk in front of a camera.

God could have given this platform to anyone, but for some reason he chose me. It reminds me of my favorite verse, Jeremiah 29:11, which says, "'For I know the plans I have for you,' declares the Lord, 'plans to prosper you and not to harm you, plans to give you hope and a future.'"

As I've gone through the ups and downs of being a social media influencer, I've seen how much I need the hope and a future this verse talks about. And as I've heard from my subscribers, I *know* that my generation is desperate for the hope and future that Christ can offer them.

Standing on that stage in LA as a fourteen-year-old, I had no idea the plan God had for me and my budding YouTube channel. Almost six years later, I'm amazed at what he has done. I have learned that God is the author and inventor of beauty in all areas of my life. He is beautiful when the world is ugly. And life is truly beautiful when I walk through it with him.

XOXO,

Chels

Insider Beauty Tip:

DEMYSTIFYING CURLING IRONS

I've had long hair for most of my life, and it took some time to figure out the easiest way to curl it. I passed on my knowledge in one of my early videos, "How I Curl My Hair ♥." The first step to great curls is choosing the right curling iron. Here's how to pick the right one:

Big-Barrel Iron: This curling iron works great on longer hair to create looser, wavier curls. Try facing the clamp of your curling iron forward to spin the hair through it more easily, and clamp around the middle of your hair. Clamping hair from the bottom of the strand makes it harder and more awkward to curl around the iron.

Medium-Barrel Iron: Use this iron to create full, bouncy curls. More defined curls can be great for updos. Remember to the rule "root to tip": the closer to the root you start the curl, the longer the curl will last.

Small-Barrel Iron: If you have shoulder-length hair or shorter, you'll want to choose a small-barreled curling iron to define your curls. Point the iron downward as you curl. Tighter curls on the underside of your hair will also help your do have more volume.

CHAPTER 2

IN REAL LIFE

Beauty begins the moment you decide to be yourself.

—COCO CHANEL

When I was ten, I dreamed of being an Olympic gymnast. That was the year Shawn Johnson won gold on the balance beam and Nastia Liukin claimed individual all-around champion at the summer games. As a young girl, I was mesmerized by these beautiful, talented young women and I wanted to be just like them.

I started taking gymnastics when I was nine years old. At first, I did great. I mastered skills at a steady rate and kept up with the other girls in my class. By my third year, I could do a handspring onto the vault and a round-off back handspring tumbling pass. That's when things started to change. I noticed the girls around me learning higher-level skills while I stayed consistent or even lost ground.

They added a back tuck (backflip) and even a back twist to their tumbling passes, while I struggled to do a back tuck, period. On the bars, the other girls could swing their bodies up and around with ease, while

I just tried to hold on. And my balance beam cartwheels were an epic fail—half the time, I ended up splitting the beam and hurting myself and my pride.

When I first noticed my skills slipping, I resolved to try harder. I watched the girls who were excelling and attempted to follow their example. But after a few months of taking people's advice and working hard without seeing results, I became frustrated and started getting down on myself. Did I have what it took? Was there any point in continuing?

Even at ten years old, watching my dreams of Olympic glory begin to fade was a terrible feeling. It hurts when you realize you're not going to have the future you envisioned and that there's nothing you can do about it. By the end of the summer before my freshman year of high school, I was burnt out, and it had become clear it was time to call it quits as a gymnast. As hard as it was to accept that I wasn't going to be the next Shawn Johnson, I knew leaving gymnastics was the right decision. God had other plans for me; I just didn't know what they were yet.

THAT CELEBRITY LIFE

When I first started my YouTube channel, nothing changed at first. I was still a regular teen living in a small town, attending school like everyone else, and going to as many high school football games as I could. I never really had a desire to be famous. And I had no idea that my channel would take off the way it did.

Flying to Los Angeles for the NYX Face Awards was my first real taste of the celebrity lifestyle. I stayed in a fancy hotel, a chauffeur drove me and my friend Charis to the NYX headquarters, and I received a one-on-one makeup session with celebrity makeup artist Scott Barnes.

After the competition, I started receiving more of the perks that came with having a recognized YouTube channel. Companies showered me with free makeup and products, hoping I'd talk about them in my videos. I was featured in newspaper and magazine articles, invited to attend national conventions, and even asked to speak at youth events. The attention and opportunities were exhilarating . . . and a little daunting!

My biggest challenge was the pressure of constantly having to create videos and content, even if I was going through something hard in my life or felt like I needed a break. But the real struggle at first was that it really bothered me when people posted unkind things. I had to develop a thick skin. I tried to remember that these people didn't actually know me—they were just judging based on a video or how I dressed. I could choose to not allow their opinions to bother me. So that's what I did.

BALANCING LIFE AND YOUTUBE

As my career began to accelerate, I realized running a YouTube channel was going to be a lot of work. A fan may watch a five-minute video on my channel and think that my life is totally glamorous and fun. It *is* a lot

of fun, but what they don't know is that each video requires up to two hours of filming and sometimes twice that amount of time to edit, which I do myself.

On top of the filming and editing, I have to plan upcoming content, upload videos, post regularly on social media, consider different offers, and respond to emails. So one way that I was becoming *different* from a normal teenage girl was that I was putting in eighteen to twenty hours of work each week to produce the content my subscribers enjoyed. I had unwittingly created a part-time job for myself—one where I was my own boss and sometimes made up the rules as I went.

I also had to go to school, keep my grades up, spend time with my family and friends, and squeeze in other interests in my spare time. Sometimes my life was exhausting, and many times I just didn't feel like putting in the work needed to make the videos and meet the strenuous content demands. I wasn't an expert on keeping balance in my life—as evidenced by my balance beam fails—and it started to show.

My struggle to balance all the pieces of my life came to a head during my junior year. That year I attended eight events across the nation, filmed my own online TV show, and appeared in a reality TV show with my family, all while producing regular content for my channel and going to school. I was busy, to say the least!

My friends started saying, "Chelsea, we haven't talked to you in forever. We never see you anymore. Every weekend, you're in a different state." I realized they were right. YouTube was consuming my life. I knew that if I kept up my breakneck pace of life, I would end up sacrificing relationships and the normal teen experiences that really mattered to me.

STEPPING BACK

When I realized my life was racing in a direction I didn't necessarily want it to go, I took a step back and did some self-evaluation. The first thing I had to do was to decide what I wanted my life to be about, so I made a mental list of my priorities.

CHELSEA'S THUMBS UP
AND THUMBS DOWN

FOOD
👍 Thumbs up: Taco salad
👎 Thumbs down: Broccoli

THEME PARK RIDES
👍 Thumbs up: The Superman at Six Flags St. Louis—a ride that drops you at the top of a tower
👎 Thumbs down: The X-Calibur—a ride that spins, goes upside down and around and around, until you want to throw up and die

MOVIES
👍 Thumbs up: Any Nicholas Sparks movie
👎 Thumbs down: Any sci-fi movie

MUSIC STYLES
👍 Thumbs up: EVERYTHING!
👎 Thumbs down: But no screamo or hard rock

BEAUTY TOOL
👍 Thumbs up: I love a nice fluffy brush for applying blush.
👎 Thumbs down: Beauty blender—though a lot of people swear by these, I think brushes work better.

MY QUIRKS
👍 Thumbs up: I am super adaptable to any situation.
👎 Thumbs down: Although I like sarcasm, sometimes I don't take it the right way.

GIFT FROM A FAN
👍 Thumbs up: I once received a huge box of foreign candy!
👎 Thumbs down: I appreciate everything, but I wish everyone included their social media info when they write to me, so I can let them know I received it and loved it!

SPORT
👍 Thumbs up: Dance, tennis, and watching football
👎 Thumbs down: Golf and bowling

SCHOOL SUBJECT
👍 Thumbs up: I love English and the chance to write about something I love!
👎 Thumbs down: I absolutely dread math.

FASHION LOOK
👍 Thumbs up: I love wearing flannels around my waist.
👎 Thumbs down: I'm not a big fan of platform shoes; I don't find them flattering.

My faith in Christ. At the beginning of high school, I'd given my life fully to Jesus Christ, so I knew I wanted to make my relationship with him my number one priority. That meant I needed to spend time with him daily and attend church and youth group, where I could receive encouragement from other believers. I noticed that when I wasn't spending regular time in God's Word and in prayer, I just didn't feel like myself.

I committed to starting most days with a quiet time of Bible study and prayer. I found that spending that time with God set the tone for how I treated people or reacted to stressful situations throughout the day. I sometimes missed my moment first thing in the morning, but I always tried to do it by the end of the day.

My family and friends. I decided that another priority was my relationships. Even though I had millions of online contacts, I was grateful for the people in my everyday life and realized I needed to put them before my work. These were the people who had been with me all along, the ones who would be there long after my YouTube career ended. For a long time, I've tried to keep this saying in mind: "Love God, love people, and love what you do." Those three things should always be in that order.

To make sure I had time for family and friends, I set realistic goals for my YouTube content. I did the work to post two videos a week, but the rest of the time I focused on people. I tried to set aside one day during the weekend to spend time with my friends, and I committed to going to church on Sunday and to youth group during the week.

I was also intentional about the YouTube events I chose to do. I said no to certain opportunities so I could keep my normal life and invest in the people I cared about the most. While I didn't always balance everything perfectly—and sometimes I still don't—I did see God blessing the choices I'd made by growing my relationships with family and friends.

My work. With a regular job, no matter what is going on in your life, you still have to go to work. But as someone in business for myself, I'm in control of when I work and how much I work. I've discovered it takes a lot of self-discipline to work on videos or post on social media when I'm feeling tired, lazy, or uninspired . . . or would rather be doing something else.

At first, I struggled to be diligent in my work. But during the past few years, I've come to realize that work—and specifically what I'm doing through my YouTube channel—is one of the most important parts of myself. My top goals are to love God and love people. But one of the ways I do that is by loving what I do and taking joy in accomplishing the work God has called me to.

As soon as I really started to understand the platform God had given me, it became easier to want to do my work consistently. There are still times when I don't feel motivated or want to do something else with my time, but I remind myself of the reasons I do what I do.

Once I had established my priorities, I made a plan to get everything done. Anyone who knows me will tell you that I love routine. I mean, I really, *really* love it. Structure is my friend, and I'm most comfortable when there's a natural routine and things to accomplish each day. During summer break, I always had to work at it, but I still tried to keep some kind of schedule so I could get things done (and keep my sanity).

As part of my renewed passion to live the life I wanted and to focus on my priorities, I used a calendar and started planning ahead. A calendar allowed me to see what I needed to do each day, and also reminded me of events coming up that I was looking forward to, such as spending time at a friend's house or going to the football game.

Building structure into my life and making a plan for accomplishing the things I needed to do relieved a lot of stress that had come from taking on every opportunity that came my way. As I let the less important things go and made time for the more important, I found the balance I needed to be healthy and productive.

HOW TO CREATE A GREAT ROUTINE

My routine videos on YouTube are some of my most popular. And it's no wonder! People are always looking for ways to be more productive and do things in less time. Here are some ways to create your own killer routine:

Consider your daily schedule and priorities. I like to do this weekly or monthly. Think about the things that will fill your time during the next week or month. I first try to schedule what matters to me the most. For example, I always begin my day with some quiet time with God.

Stay on task. Each night, I make a to-do list for the following day. I recommend numbering the items in order of importance, so you know which ones to tackle first and which ones can wait until another day if you run out of time. At the end of the day, evaluate how it went and make adjustments for the next day. (Note: I like to pick up cute to-do lists at variety stores, because they make me feel more motivated to use them!)

Use a calendar. I hang a calendar in my room and write upcoming events and special days on it. Then I cross off the days and look over what's coming up. Seeing the things I have to look forward to helps me keep a positive outlook when there's a lot on my plate.

Give yourself a break. A routine can feel limiting at times, or like a lot of work. It's important to plan downtime into your routine. Whether you enjoy taking a run, taking a nap (my favorite!), or just taking a few minutes to sit down and read, leave space in your day for things you enjoy.

KEEPING IT REAL

Anytime someone asks me "What is it like to be famous?", I don't know how to answer, mainly because I don't *feel* famous. When BeautyLiciousInsider passed 1.5 million subscribers and was ranked among the top 1,600 of all YouTube channels, I was still living a life similar to the one I'd always had.

Growing up, I was the normal kid who played hopscotch on the sidewalk with the neighbor kids and ran lemonade stands with my siblings. (My parents bought most of the product, because who wants to buy a cup of kid-touched lemonade?) I was drawn to sports and outdoor activities and spent a lot of time with my siblings.

Once I started my YouTube channel, life remained pretty much the same, for the most part. Growing up in such a small town helped keep me grounded and connected to the people I cared about. There's a huge sense of community in a small town. Everyone knows each other, and you have a support system that's like an extended family. I love that the kids I grew up with are still my best friends.

As my YouTube channel grew, I didn't want to get swept into some fake celebrity existence. So I stayed very involved in my school by joining the tennis team, serving on student council, and taking a video production class during my senior year. Every Friday night, our school had a football game, and I made it a point to go. Some of my best high

school memories revolve around those games and going out with friends afterward. I went to countless bonfires and game nights, and tried not to say no to invitations to hang out with people I cared about.

I invited my friends to participate in what I was doing with my YouTube channel—and sometimes my friends would join me in a video—but I also respected their privacy. Not everyone wants to be online. I was careful about how I talked about my friends and my boyfriend, careful what I shared with the world. I discovered that every conversation doesn't need to be quoted on Twitter. Every picture doesn't need to be posted on Instagram. My friends and family members trusted that I wouldn't share their secrets online, and it allowed us to have deeper relationships.

FAMOUS FOR HIM

Like I said before, I have never thought of myself as famous. I'm still surprised when someone recognizes me in public and asks for a picture. I'm not famous. I just have a job that happens to be on the Internet, and have gained a following of people who like what I talk about. I am very aware that my work isn't what's gotten me here—God's faithfulness has. As I've followed him, he's blessed the work that I'm doing.

Being an influence in young women's lives and sharing my faith in Christ online is exciting work! I wake up every day in anticipation of what God is going to do. I have been blessed with opportunities to collaborate with amazing, positive people and show that Christ's presence is on the Internet.

I have heard my generation referred to as "digital natives," because we never knew life without computers and the Internet. Sometimes I forget that people haven't always been so connected. The Internet ushered in a new way for people to share ideas, as well as avenues to share one's faith. In the past, people had to go to churches, listen to the radio, or read books to learn more about God. Now billions of people from nearly every country in the world can log on to watch a video or read a blog post and hear about Jesus! That's why I have such a passion for what I do.

In the end, I'm glad I never became an Olympic gymnast. God didn't create me for that. Instead, he had plans to use me for exactly who I am, at this moment in history. There was a time where I felt like I was giving up the future I wanted for myself, but it doesn't even compare to the future God had for me.

XOXO,

Chels

Insider Beauty Tip:

CREATING A NATURAL FACE

For me, part of being real—and showing who I am—is not wearing heavy makeup all the time. Whether it's summertime or you're just wanting a simple look to reveal your natural beauty, here are a few tips to create a make-under look that rocks:

1. Start with a BB cream to protect your skin and to cover up minor imperfections. Stay away from heavy concealers or foundation.
2. Add a touch of eyeliner on your lower lids (I like blue) and mascara.
3. Apply a light-colored lip stain for all-day staying power or a gloss for shine.
4. Use a clean powder to set the look and reduce oily shine.

CHAPTER 3

LIVING FOR SOMETHING BIGGER

How beautiful are the feet of those who bring good news!

ROMANS 10:15

Have you ever noticed that the best conversations happen after midnight?

That was the case for me as I sat in a darkened room with three of my best friends, our pillows and sleeping bags strewn across the floor. We were attending a Christian youth event at our church, and God was speaking to all of our hearts in a big way.

In the early hours of the morning, we began sharing some of the difficult things each of us were going through. One girl was anxious because her parents were having issues in their marriage. Several of us felt pressure to do things we knew were wrong in order to feel accepted. One girl talked about her struggles with wanting attention and validation from guys.

Even though we were all going through different hardships, we realized that we all needed God in a big way. At one point, I said, "You guys, we need to pray for each other. Right now." For the next hour, we poured out our hearts to God as we prayed about the hard things going on in our lives. We asked God to help us to stay strong and to honor him through the problems we were facing, and to draw us together as friends so that we could encourage each other.

I will never forget that night; God ignited a spark in my heart to know him better. I realized my life would never be the same, and I was filled with anticipation and peace that I had never known before.

FAITH LIKE A CHILD

You may be wondering why I'm talking about God all of a sudden when I'm known for giving beauty advice. Well, like you, I'm a lot of different things, and one of those things is a Christian. So I don't know who you are or what you believe right now, but I want to share this part of my story with you. Faith isn't always easy to talk about, and it's definitely not easy to live it out in daily life. That's why it's so important to me to share what I believe. I hope that no matter where you are in life right now, you'll see the amazing things God has done in my life, and that maybe it will cause you to think about what he could do in yours.

My testimony isn't that different from a lot of Christian kids out

there. I grew up in a Christian family, and we attended church on Sundays. I remember accepting Christ while I was in the bathtub. (I know; weird, right?) I was ten, and the realization that I needed Jesus to forgive my sins and come into my life just clicked in my young brain. I told my mom, "I think I want to give my life to God."

After that, my life didn't change a whole lot. I believed in Jesus, but I pretty much lived like anyone else my age. I didn't get in trouble during middle school, but I didn't make decisions based on Christ's teachings either. I struggled with friendships and finding acceptance. I did things to please those around me instead of God.

By the beginning of my freshman year of high school, I knew my life wasn't working. Drama seemed to surround me at school, at dance class, and even at home sometimes. I wasn't attending church during this time, and I was tired of trying to manage life in my own way. That's when some friends and I attended a Christian youth event called DNow. The point of the weekend was to help teens learn what it means to be a disciple of Jesus.

(If you're like me, the word *disciple* may make you think of a guy with a beard who wears sandals and a robe. But the Bible says that everyone who loves and follows Christ is his disciple, or follower. Being a disciple means trying to walk in Jesus' footsteps and simply being with him.)

The speaker at the conference talked about leaving the past behind and pressing into what God had in store for us next. What he said really spoke to me. I felt like he was specifically talking about my life. Although I believed in God, I didn't have a close, meaningful relationship with him. I realized I couldn't just sit back and expect my life to magically change. I needed to invest in my relationship with God as I would with any other person.

In any relationship, you get out of it what you put in. For example, when you like someone, you don't want to see him only once a week. You don't say, "Okay, I'm going to go on a two-hour date with you on Sunday, and then I won't talk to you again until next Sunday." What kind of relationship would that be? And yet that's exactly what we sometimes do with God. I was beginning to see that having a relationship with him wasn't about following a list of dos and don'ts, but it was about getting to know him and growing in my love for him.

When I realized that being a Christian was about having a relationship, my life really began to change. I found myself wanting to read my Bible and talk to God—even about little things. I still had struggles and challenges in my life, but now I had a friend and Father who I knew loved me and wanted what was best for me at all times.

THE BIG LIE

When I was younger, even though I knew about Jesus, I believed some things that weren't true. I believed that my worth came from how I looked or what I did, and that if I didn't do the right things or look the right way, people wouldn't like me. I also believed that what I wanted and the plans I had for myself were best. And since my life was pretty good, I didn't realize that God had something so much better for me.

When we're going through life without God, we may think that certain things—such as money, a party lifestyle, and popularity—will make us happy and fulfilled. But more often than not, those superficial things only make us feel more empty and miserable. Some people may even tell us to do anything and everything we want when we want it, because "YOLO"—you only live once.

It's true that you only live once, but the Bible is clear that our life on this earth is short compared to eternity. And what we choose to do here—and who we choose to spend time with—matters after we die. Yes, we should pursue our dreams. Yes, we should enjoy our time on earth. But we should always be thinking about whether our choices and our actions are taking us down the right path.

Jesus told us that he is the light of the world. When we walk with him, we will never walk in darkness. We have a choice to make about how we will act and who we will follow—and how we will shine Jesus' light in the world. I've found that no matter how bad things get, there are always opportunities to be that light. Sometimes I've faced criticism over things I've posted on YouTube. People's unkind or unfair comments can get me down and make me feel like what I'm doing doesn't matter. But over time I've realized that in a place where people often tear others down, it's even more important for me to shine brightly, and to be loving and kind.

And the Internet isn't the only place where negativity and hurt lives, of course. I'm sure you've had the feeling that something is not right with our world. We see hate and violence and selfishness all over the place. People get sick and die. Terrible things happen to good people, and good things happen to terrible people. None of it seems right or fair.

Watching the 24-hour news cycle filled with awful people and events would be super depressing, except we know that there's also love and compassion and beauty in this world! We see that beauty when we experience random acts of kindness from strangers, watch a gorgeous sunrise, or get a heartfelt hug from a friend. We long for those things to make our lives complete, but the best way to experience beauty and meaning in this life is to have a relationship with Christ.

CHASING BEAUTY

So what is the answer? How can we have the good in our lives instead of the bad? How can life be more than living for the moment and the approval of others?

As I mentioned in earlier chapters, being a part of BeautyLicious Insider has shown me that God has even better plans for us than what we can plan for ourselves. I think that's amazing! Someone loves us and has good things planned for our lives. Even when things get hard and the bad seems to be taking over, we can know God is there guiding us toward the future he has planned for us. In fact, every time I doubt myself, I go back to Jeremiah 29:11; it's a reminder that God is always at my side and wants what's best for me. Last year, my plans for myself changed dramatically when I wasn't able to go to college as I had planned. Even though those months were some of the hardest of my life, I watched God bring so much good out of what felt really bad at the time.

LIVING REAL LIFE

When I accepted Jesus into my life as a ten-year-old, I didn't totally get what that meant. I didn't understand I needed to seek him daily, and that he needed to be the number one relationship in my life. I heard those things at church, but I didn't really take them in. The ups and downs of my daily life and what other people thought were still more important to me.

When I *committed* my whole life to Christ at the beginning of my freshman year of high school, my life began to change. I quickly realized

HOW TO HAVE A RELATIONSHIP WITH CHRIST

Whether you're just beginning to explore your faith or you accepted Jesus into your life years ago, it's always good to remember the basics. Use the tips below to grow in your faith every day.

- Get to know the story of Jesus by reading the Bible. (I recommend starting with the book of Mark!)
- Talk to friends and family members who are Christians. Ask them about their faith and how it has changed their lives.
- Pray. There's no special way to pray—God knows your heart and always wants to hear your voice! You can say the words out loud, think them in your mind, or write them down.
- Go to church or youth group. Get to know the community of believers in your area, and notice the ways they are serving each other and those in the community.
- Speak with a church leader. When you're just starting out in your relationship with Christ, you may have some big questions. A church leader (like a pastor or youth leader) can help answer those questions.

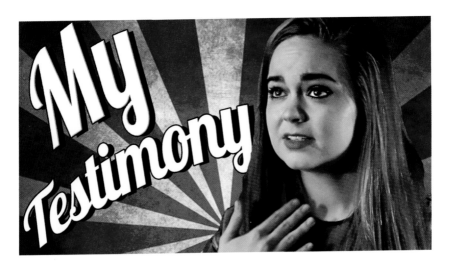

My Testimony

that I needed to align all of my decisions with him; I couldn't just pick and choose when to be a Christian. I had to give him every area of my life.

I began spending time with friends who would encourage me in my faith, and cut out relationships that were a bad influence on me. I attended church and youth group to be around other Christians. And I started waking up early to read my Bible and pray for a few minutes before school. As I did these things, God began to grow in me a love and passion for him that I wanted to share with others.

I posted a video of my testimony on my YouTube channel, explaining my decision to follow Jesus, what God meant to me, and how he was changing me. Hundreds of my subscribers left comments, saying how the video had encouraged them and asking me to make more videos about faith. As a result, I posted additional videos to help my subscribers get to know God better and know how to live for him.

As I saw how the faith videos were helping people, something occurred to me: God had been planning to use my YouTube channel in this way all along. I had started my channel for fun, but he was turning it into something different—something with a bigger purpose. I suddenly had the opportunity to share my faith with thousands of people. Of course, there was some pushback. Some of my fans didn't appreciate me "pushing my religion" on them, but I decided to do what God was asking of me and not worry about losing subscribers over it.

Even after I began speaking up about my faith in Christ, my channel continued to grow. I was far from perfect—and I made sure my subscribers knew that—but God was changing my heart and giving me a growing passion for him.

THE ATTACK

You may be thinking that once I had this amazing encounter with Jesus, I never struggled again. I was suddenly this super-Christian who never did anything wrong. Not true. Even when my Christian life is going great, and I feel pretty strong, an attack on my faith can still take me by surprise! Attacks like this can happen to any of us when life gets busy or stressful, when we're feeling insecure, or when we're just not spending much time with God.

I've had a few big attacks on my faith—along with a lot of little ones (and do on a daily basis, it sometimes seems). One big attack happened during my junior year of high school. I began to have doubts about whether God's ways were best, and I was curious about the things some of my friends were doing. My first bad decision was to date a guy who was a bad influence. (My parents didn't want me to date him, so it also caused a lot of tension between us.) He talked casually about things like drinking and drugs. While I was dating him, I went to a few parties where people were drinking and making other unwise choices, and what I saw around me didn't seem so bad. In fact, the things they were doing seemed enticing and fun!

Despite our best intentions, no one is immune to the allure of temptation. But I discovered that although those parties were fun and exciting in the moment, the choices I made there stole the sense of peace and safety I had in Christ and left me with shame and regret. Giving into temptation killed some of the good things God had been doing in my heart.

Maybe you've experienced something similar. You talked badly about a friend behind her back and ruined the friendship. You went too far with your boyfriend. You lied to your parents. You blew up at your sibling. You didn't stand up for someone who was being bullied. You *were* the bully.

If we each made a list of our mistakes, every list would be different. But we would find we have one thing in common: we *all* screw up. God calls it sin. And while that might just sound like some religious word, one that makes you think of being judged or not being good enough, the Bible says that it's the root of all of our problems. And we've all done it. (Romans 3:23 confirms it.) The good news is Jesus, who died to pay for every sin we will ever do, is a friend of imperfect people. He loves you no matter what you have done. He promises to help us say no to temptation, because he knows we will be better off when we don't get dragged down by it.

After a few months of living a life that I knew didn't honor Christ, I realized I didn't have peace. I thought, *What am I doing? I don't want to be living this lifestyle. It's not me. There's a reason I'm a Christian.* God woke me up and reminded me that he had saved me for a purpose. I felt ashamed of the way I had been living, and I knew God had a much better path for me. I had been missing out on his plan because I chose to do things that put a wedge between us.

When I decided to turn away from that lifestyle and live for Jesus again, it wasn't as easy as I thought it would be. I still got offers to go to parties, and sometimes I was tempted. I knew I needed backup. I told my parents what had happened, and I also chose to hang out with friends I knew would encourage me in my faith instead of leading me toward bad decisions. I started going back to church and youth group, something I had avoided when I wasn't living for God.

Although my earlier choices brought pain and regret, I learned something: Sometimes our worst downfalls can be new beginnings with God. He never runs out of grace. He even has compassion on us when we are suffering because of *our own bad choices*! Nothing can separate us from his love. Despite my poor decisions, I knew God welcomed me back with open arms.

THE BIG FIVE

One thing I've become passionate about as I've learned to walk with God is getting to know him better. The Christian life is a process. Going back to the example of a romantic relationship, when you really like someone, you don't just see that person once a week. You want to spend every minute with him, and you always want to get to know him better!

The same is true with God. At first, it may seem weird to have a "relationship" with God. But I've found that the more I get to know him, the more amazed I am by who he is and how he loves me. He is constantly teaching me new things, and having a relationship with him is never boring!

Here are five main ways I develop my relationship with God:

Bible reading: The Bible is one of the central ways that God speaks to us. He used forty different authors, who were inspired by the Holy Spirit, to write the sixty-six books of Scripture. Every morning I try to spend time reading the Bible. I usually read through a few verses or a chapter at a time. I like to take notes about what I read and write down any questions that come to mind.

The Bible is "alive and active," which means that even though some of it may be hard to understand, it totally applies to our lives and what we're going through. I love how when I read Scripture in the morning, many times those verses apply directly to something that happens during my day. More than once, God has used a verse to encourage me or give me strength at just the right time.

Tip: Try a Bible reading plan—easily searchable online—to read through the entire Bible in a year.

Obedience: There's a verse in James that says, "Do not merely listen to the word, and so deceive yourselves. Do what it says" (James 1:22). Just reading the Bible is not enough; to have a true relationship with Christ, we also need to obey what the Bible tells us. And when we obey what Jesus tells us to do, we show that we love him and respect his authority in our lives.

I've discovered that the rules in the Bible are intended for my happiness and joy. Obedience shows that I trust that God's ways are better than my own. It's not always easy to obey, that's for sure. But when I do, life always seems to turn out better, even when I don't see it right away.

Tip: Take notes while you do your Bible reading and jot down specific ways you could put what you're reading about into practice.

Prayer: Think of the person you talk to the most. Is it your mom? A sister? Your best friend? Talking to someone is a big part of having a relationship. And prayer is a big part of having a relationship with God. I think of it as a continual conversation with him.

I like to pray before I read the Bible, asking God to help me understand his Word and show me how to apply it to my life. When I make a poor choice, I pray for forgiveness. I also pray for help when I'm facing a challenge, and say a prayer of thanks when something good happens. I love that I can pray to God at any time about anything and know that he always hears me. He may not answer in the way I would like, but I can trust that he hears and will answer.

Tip: Set an alarm on your phone for the same time each day. Choose a time when you're available, like in the afternoon when school is over. When the alarm goes off, take five minutes to reconnect with God through prayer.

Church: Going to church isn't a requirement for being a Christian, but God does want us to meet together with other believers. Church isn't just a building where we go to sing pretty songs and hear a sermon. Every Christian in the world is part of God's larger church. It is something that connects every believer.

Church is a great place to meet other Christians who can encourage you in your commitment to Christ. When I think back on times when I attended church and youth group regularly and times when I didn't, I was always stronger in my faith and more passionate about Christ when I was meeting regularly with other Christians. For me, going to church is a way I put God first in my life.

Tip: Go with a friend. Church can be a little overwhelming when you attend alone. Going with a friend or family member can give you accountability and someone to sit with!

Outreach: A few years ago, I was able to go on a mission trip to Alaska with my friend Charis (the winner of the NYX Face Awards). It was life-changing. We served out in the middle of "the bush" in Alaska, where we helped lead a summer camp for elementary-school-aged kids. Many of them lived in the tiny villages nearby, and it was incredible to see them come to know Christ and grow closer to him.

One of our jobs as Christians is to help people develop a relationship with Christ. One way I've tried to do this is by making YouTube videos that support my subscribers as they grow in their faith. Church also provides a lot of opportunities to get involved and serve as well.

Tip: Look into the ministry opportunities your church offers and pick one to get involved in.

FIVE WAYS TO GET MORE
OUT OF BIBLE READING

Although it may not seem too exciting to read a book written over two thousand years ago, reading the Bible doesn't have to feel like a chore. Here are five ways to enhance your time in God's Word:

1. **Start with the New Testament.** The Old Testament is great, but some parts of it are hard to understand. If you're new to the Bible, try starting with the book of Mark, which is easy to read and takes you through the life and death of Jesus.

2. **Pray.** Say a simple prayer like this one before you read: "God, I may not be able to fully understand what your Word means, but I am eager to hear from you. You have my full attention, Lord. Speak to me."

3. **Tackle a few verses at a time.** If your reading goals are too ambitious, you may not end up reading at all. I usually read a few verses at a time. Try for three or four at first, and then work your way up.

4. **Take notes.** I love to interact with what I'm reading. If I read something interesting, I may underline it in my Bible or write a note in the margin. I also use a notebook and write down questions I have or observations on how I can apply the verses to my life.

5. **Do it every day.** I have found that for me, the best time to study the Bible is first thing in the morning. Starting my day in God's Word sets the tone for my whole day and gives me the right perspective. Some people love to read right before bed. Choose a time each day that is best for you, and then stick with it!

WINNING THE FIGHT

Something I've learned since becoming a Christian is that faith is an ongoing process made up of daily decisions. Life doesn't get easier just because you know Christ: The hard times still come. Relationships still get broken. You still make plenty of mistakes and face many temptations. The difference is, you have a friend who will never leave you as you walk through those hard things. He even knows what it feels like, because he came to earth in human form and experienced every emotion and temptation that we do.

I still think about the things I heard the weekend I fully committed my life and future to Jesus. Some of them were from Philippians 3:13–14, where the apostle Paul says, "Brothers and sisters, I do not consider myself yet to have taken hold of it. But one thing I do: Forgetting what is behind and straining toward what is ahead, I press on toward the goal to win the prize for which God has called me heavenward in Christ Jesus."

None of us are perfect. We haven't arrived at our final destination. There is always more to learn and do on this journey with Jesus. Faith is a process. But it is also a great adventure.

XOXO,

Chels

Insider Beauty Tip:

FOUNDATIONAL BEAUTY

My faith is the true foundation of my life. But when it comes to beauty, there are a few foundational things you can do to look good without much work. Here are a few of my tricks:

- Your eyebrows frame your features, so keep them groomed. I like to get my eyebrows shaped about once a month. Then I use tweezers to maintain.
- Exfoliate your skin twice a week to slough away dead skin, and use a detox mask at least once a week to keep skin glowing.
- Take a fish oil supplement to give your hair a natural shine.
- If you use nail polish, remove it whenever it becomes chipped and old.
- Get your hair trimmed or cut every one to three months, depending on length and/or how high-mantainance your hairstyle is. A fresh cut removes split ends and keeps you looking neat and stylish.

CHAPTER 4

FREE TO BE ME

Beauty without grace is the hook without the bait.

—RALPH WALDO EMERSON

I used to scroll through my Instagram feed and see picture after picture of the beautiful models and artists I followed, and I felt kind of insignificant in comparison.

Social media is a blessing and a curse. On one hand, it's a really fun place to connect with friends and gain new ideas. (And, obviously, what I do depends on it!) I love following and being inspired by other beauty vloggers. Though on the other hand, social media bombards us with perfect images that can convince us we don't measure up.

Recently, it seems like society is starting to move away from the one, stick-thin body type as its ideal of beauty, and I'm glad. But the media still pushes certain looks at us. We still see lots of trim, perfectly proportioned bodies and clear, glowing faces staring back at us in those images. If you don't fit "the look," it can be easy to feel as if you're not pretty enough.

While younger women may feel this pressure more strongly, surveys have shown that age doesn't necessarily change how women perceive themselves. A few years ago, Dove's Self-Esteem Project interviewed

6,400 women ages eighteen to sixty-four from around the world. While 80 percent of the women surveyed said that all women had something beautiful about them, 96 percent said they wouldn't use the word "beautiful" to describe themselves. How sad!

I guess it's no surprise that with all the perfection we see online and in the media, most of us feel imperfect in some way—especially when it comes to the way we look. We're flooded with ads for quick weight loss methods and products to give us clear skin or perfect hair. This can make us feel like we need to fix ourselves, so we begin the endless search for the next thing that will make us feel beautiful.

TWO STANDARDS OF BEAUTY

The world makes a big deal about outward appearance. Magazines feature the "most beautiful" people on their covers. Actors receive a lot of attention for gaining (or losing) weight, changing their hairstyles, or wearing sweatpants in public (the horror!). And models often have to maintain an unrealistic physique to keep getting jobs—and when they get a job, they are sometimes airbrushed beyond recognition.

Judging each other based on outward appearance is nothing new. There's a story in the Old Testament where God told the prophet Samuel to anoint the next king of Israel. God sent him to the house of Jesse, a man who had eight sons. Samuel looked at Jesse's oldest son, Eliab, and thought for sure he was the next king. Tall and handsome, Eliab looked the part. But God had different plans.

1 Samuel 16:7–8 says, "But the Lord said to Samuel, 'Do not consider his appearance or his height, for I have rejected him. The Lord does not look at the things people look at. People look at the outward appearance, but the Lord looks at the heart.'"

After that, Jesse brought each of his next six sons before Samuel, but none of them was the king. Finally, Jesse brought his youngest son in from the field, where he was taking care of sheep. His name was David. Then God told Samuel, "Rise and anoint him; this is the one."

God's standard of beauty is so opposite of the world's. He looks at our hearts. He says that you are created in his image and that you are accepted and loved exactly the way you are—the way he made you. There are no rules; no picture to copy. And the best part is, he never makes a mistake!

When I realized I didn't have to fit into a cardboard cutout of the perfect individual—with the right hair, face, and body shape—it was such a relief. I'm accepted and loved for exactly who I am! God looks at what's inside. He sees my heart—my strength and love and kindness. He

finds me beautiful whether I'm dressed up for a special event or sporting bedhead on a Saturday morning. That is so reassuring.

No one in the world is exactly like you. No one has your eyes, your smile, or your personality. When you quit trying to follow the world's rules for beauty and realize that God sees you and loves you for who you really are, it takes a lot of pressure away.

Through my experiences with YouTube, I've learned that the beauty industry is a competitive and fickle place. I can never win at the outward-beauty game; there will always be someone more beautiful than I am. So although it can feel like attaining a certain level of beauty will make me happy and fulfilled, I know it never will. That's because the things I'm truly yearning for—unconditional love and acceptance—are things that come from God.

FINDING YOUR BEAUTIFUL

We've already established that God thinks you're beautiful. He made you and he loves all of your details. But your version of beautiful is going to look different from mine, which is going to look a lot different from the most beautiful Hollywood actress at the moment. That can be hard to accept, because it's so natural to compare ourselves to others.

Here's how it works: I scroll through my Instagram feed and see all of these perfect-looking people and their perfect-looking lives. I see people who are more beautiful than me. People who are having more fun than me. People who have a lot more stuff than I do. And I even see people who seem to have a better relationship with God than I have. Comparison is destructive, because it steals my gratefulness for the amazing things God is doing in my life. It makes me envy others instead of love them.

Not long ago, a couple I follow through social media (who are about my age) got engaged. I was happy for them, but I also felt a lot of jealousy—I wished *I* was the one madly in love and getting engaged. Later, I realized that what I saw on social media was *their* story. God was writing a different story for me. I needed to stop comparing my life to someone else's social media account.

Getting out of the comparison trap requires shifting your focus. Instead of filling your mind with what's in your Instagram and Snapchat feeds, you have to fill your mind with what God is calling you to do today.

I'm really encouraged by the words of Hebrews 12:1–2, which say, "Therefore . . . let us run with perseverance the race marked out for us, fixing our eyes on Jesus, the pioneer and perfecter of faith."

Each of us has a specific "race" God has marked out for us. Maybe mine is a 5K and yours is a marathon. Mine may be cross-country, while yours is a road race. The cool part is, God has specifically designed your race—every twist and turn, every beautiful view, every water stop. He also made you, the runner, with specific abilities that will help you run your own race. The danger of wishing for someone else's course is that you miss out on appreciating your own race, with all of its God-designed details.

This verse also tells us to keep our eyes on Jesus, who perfects our faith. Perfection in this life is not possible apart from Jesus; he is the only one who can make us perfect. And guess what—he's never going to care if we look perfect on the outside. He cares about how we grow and become more beautiful on the inside.

When we shift our focus from looking at others to looking at Jesus, we can begin to see the ways he's created beauty in our lives. Here's something you can try: make a list of five things you like about yourself that are not physical characteristics. Here's my list:

1. I'm a goal setter.
2. I look for the best in people.
3. I can adapt to harsh situations without getting my feelings hurt.
4. I can empathize with others.
5. I work to bring unity among different groups of people.

As you make your own list, notice how it is a unique combination of traits. No one else on earth has your exact blend. That means God can use you to do things that no other person can do in exactly the way you can. Your beauty will never be duplicated in someone else.

I've noticed that as I focus on the positive things God has created in me, I'm much less likely to obsess over my imperfections. In fact, over time the negative thoughts I have about myself start to diminish. As I concentrate on growing in the areas in which God has gifted me, I don't have time to dwell on the areas where I fall short. Instead, I begin to see all that God has given me and who he has made me to be.

FIVE TIPS FOR BEING CONFIDENT

Let's face it—some days you feel more confident than others. When I feel my self-confidence fading, here are five things I do to refocus:

1. **Look the part.** I tend to feel more confident when I put on a cute dress and curl my hair in a wavy style. Maybe for you, it means wearing your favorite jeans or the boots you always receive compliments on.

2. **Exercise.** I like to go for a walk or run and listen to uplifting music to put my mind and spirit in the right place. Endorphins from running have been proven to boost your mood—plus, your jeans will fit better!

3. **Focus on others.** When I'm thinking about myself, and what others think of me, it's easy to become self-conscious. But when I think about the people around me, and how I can make their day better, I naturally feel less self-conscious and more confident.

4. **Think positive.** The messages we tell ourselves—silently or out loud—can make or break a whole day. When I'm feeling timid, I remind myself that God is with me and it's going to be a good day no matter what!

5. **Go to the source.** True confidence comes from the inside out. Psalm 71:5 says, "For you have been my hope, Sovereign Lord, my confidence since my youth." I can have full confidence in God because he will never let me down.

PEER PRESSURE AND FITTING IN

Finding your own beauty has a lot to do with deciding what kind of person you want to become. From the moment I hit seventh grade (and even earlier, if I'm really honest), I felt so much pressure to decide who I was going to be and whether or not everyone would like that version of me. That insecurity was one of the things that attracted me to makeup in the first place. I figured if I could copy the glamorous looks I saw on TV and online, I had a better chance of being accepted and liked.

One time, during middle school, I went to a friend's house for a sleepover with a bunch of other girls. I don't exactly know how it happened, but one of the girls suggested we all go skinny dipping in my friend's pool. The moment I heard the idea, I was ready to run for the hills. Skinny dipping was not something I was comfortable doing.

But before I could react, all the other girls were saying, "Oh my gosh, yes! That would be so fun!"

I didn't want to be the only one who didn't do it, and I really wanted the group to like me, so I just went along with the crowd. The entire time I was thinking, *This isn't me*, but back then I didn't have the courage to stand up and say so.

There was one person who didn't get into the pool that night. That friend, who is still a friend today, called her mom and went home early.

And you know what? It wasn't a big deal. In fact, people hardly noticed.

God spoke to me through my friend's example. I realized that I didn't want to hang out with people who pressured me into doing things I didn't want to do. And I saw that you *can* choose to do the right thing, and making that decision is not the end of the world.

WHAT IS MY LIFE BUILT ON?

Life is made up of wise and foolish decisions. I've told you about a few of my wise decisions, like accepting Christ into my life, and a few of my

WHO GOD SAYS I AM

With all of the messages coming at us through TV and social media, it's helpful to remember who God says I am. The same thing is true for you. Check out these verses that speak to our identity in Christ.

I AM A CHILD OF GOD.
So in Christ Jesus you are all children of
God through faith. Galatians 3:26

I AM A FRIEND OF JESUS.
I no longer call you servants, because a servant does
not know his master's business. Instead, I have called
you friends, for everything that I learned from my
Father I have made known to you. John 15:15

I AM A NEW CREATION.
Therefore, if anyone is in Christ, the new creation has come:
The old has gone, the new is here! 2 Corinthians 5:17

I AM ACCEPTED.
Accept one another, then, just as Christ accepted you,
in order to bring praise to God. Romans 15:7

I AM CHOSEN.
For he chose us in him before the creation of the world
to be holy and blameless in his sight. Ephesians 1:4

I HAVE ACCESS TO EVERY SPIRITUAL BLESSING.
Praise be to the God and Father of our Lord Jesus
Christ, who has blessed us in the heavenly realms with
every spiritual blessing in Christ. Ephesians 1:3

I AM A WORK OF ART.
For we are God's handiwork, created in Christ
Jesus to do good works, which God prepared
in advance for us to do. Ephesians 2:10

foolish ones, like getting involved with the wrong kinds of friends. Each kind of choice either leads you toward what God has for you or away from it.

There's a story Jesus told about two men who built houses. One of them built his house on the rock (which represents the truth of God's Word). The other man built his house on the sand. I think all of us could agree on which one sounds like a better idea.

Have you ever built a sand castle? The moment the tide comes in, it washes away the castle and changes the scene around you. Similarly, it's easy to build our lives around things other than God's Word—popularity, money, achievement, even our favorite TV shows or celebrities. But the Bible tells us that each of these things, apart from Christ, are like sand—unstable and shifting.

You may be able to guess the end of this story, but listen to what happened:

"The rain came down, the streams rose, and the winds blew and beat against that house; yet it did not fall, because it had its foundation on the rock. But everyone who hears these words of mine and does not put them into practice is like a foolish man who built his house on sand. The rain came down, the streams rose, and the winds blew and beat against that house, and it fell with a great crash" (Matthew 7:25–27).

Isn't this story like our lives? At times it feels like we are being pummeled by wind and rain. Whether it's pressure to make a bad choice or the pressure of trials in our lives—such as illness, the death of someone we love, or even just a really hard class—the storm can be overwhelming sometimes.

I don't know about you, but I want to build my life on the solid foundation of God's Word. That way, when the hard times come, I know who's holding me up and that he'll never let me fall.

That doesn't mean it's always going to be easy to live in God's truth. But if you're smart about it, there are ways you can protect yourself. Here are four walls of protection I've discovered that work to overcome peer pressure:

1. **Accountability.** One of the first things I did when I wanted to start living God's way was to end some relationships that were a bad influence. I knew I needed to be around people who would encourage me in my faith. If you're struggling with a certain temptation, confide in someone you know who would never pressure you to do wrong.

2. **Parents.** Maybe you don't have that friend who can encourage you to do what's right. I'm just going to say it: It's okay to be best friends with your parents. It may not sound cool, but God gave you your parents for a reason. They want what's best for you, and can be a great source of encouragement and help. If you don't have a close relationship with your parents, talk to a trusted family member, a teacher, a church leader, or a counselor. You'll be surprised by how understanding and supportive the adults in your life can be when you're honest with them!

3. **Church.** At times, when I've wanted to do things my own way, I've steered clear of church because I didn't want God to try to speak to me. But I've learned I *do* need to listen to what he has to say, even when it's hard, and that attending church and youth group is a great way to hear from God and stay connected with other believers. You can work together to grow in your faith and form friendships that will last through tough times.

4. **Friends.** Based on the last three points, you may be thinking that I'm advocating putting yourself inside a Christian bubble and isolating yourself from all unbelievers. I'm not saying that at all! Telling others about Jesus is a big part of being a Christian, and lots of us will have friends who don't share our exact beliefs.

My advice here is to choose your friends wisely. I fell in with a group that led to me making bad decisions, and I learned I was more susceptible to temptation if I returned to certain places or hung out with certain people. Choose friends who will build you up and support you in positive ways rather than pressure you do to something you know is wrong.

HELP MY UNBELIEF

Living my life on YouTube and social media, I sometimes have a hard time remembering that people's opinions of me—good or bad—don't really matter. God's opinion is the only one I should care about.

I'll be the first to admit that actually living that out is easier said than done. Last year I had a plan to go to an out-of-state college in the fall after I graduated from high school. I knew it was a lot to take on, considering I work up to twenty-five hours a week on my YouTube channel—and have since I was fourteen. But I wanted to have that "normal" college experience, like many of my friends, and prove to everyone that I could balance it all.

Let's just say that things did not go as planned. Within two weeks, God made it very clear that I needed to move home. At first, it felt like a major defeat, especially since I'd invited my followers to go on the journey with me, showing them the things I bought for college and giving them a tour of my dorm room. I felt as if I was letting them down. Most of my subscribers were super supportive and just concerned about me, since I was experiencing some health issues. But a few let me know that they thought I had given up too quickly and would probably regret my decision later.

I struggled to not let their words sink deep into my heart and make me feel like a failure. God had made his path for me very clear, and I knew that I was following him. I wasn't thrilled about the detour, but I

knew I needed to keep my eyes fixed on Jesus, not the idle speculation of people who only knew "YouTube me."

Even when you're doing everything you can to build your life on truth, there will be times when the winds and rain come, and you're tempted to believe a lie. It may be the lie that you're not beautiful and God somehow made a mistake. It may be the lie that the world can offer you something better than God can. Or it may be the lie that God doesn't love you or want what's best for you.

Each of these lies are destructive. As you follow Jesus, keeping your mind focused on truth will occasionally be hard. You will face tough choices, and making the right one will sometimes require huge faith. But God loves you and wants you to trust him, just like a small child trusts her father.

I'm reminded of a man who lived during the same time as Jesus. (You can read his story in Mark 9:17–29.) His son was possessed by a demon that kept throwing the boy into the fire. So the man brought his son to Jesus and asked him to help . . . "if you can."

To that, Jesus replied, "'If you can?' Everything is possible for one who believes."

Then the man replied, "I do believe; help me overcome my unbelief!"

I want to be like that man. By putting my confidence in the one who can do anything and loves me more than I can imagine, I have the ability to live in the freedom of being exactly who God made me to be—his beautiful, beloved daughter.

XOXO,

Chels

Insider Style Tip:

CHANGING UP YOUR LOOK

When I first started experimenting with makeup, I tried some crazy looks (like rainbow eye shadow.) Over the years, I've discovered what makes me feel most confident. Here are a few ways to switch up your look and feel fabulous doing it.

1. **Try a new do.** Sure, you can get a new hairstyle, but you don't have to go that drastic. If your hair is normally straight, curl it. If you normally part it on the left side, try parting it on the right. If you have naturally wavy hair, use a straightener for a sleek new look.

2. **Get out of your shopping rut.** When I go shopping, I like to have sales associates pick out outfits for me to try on. They sometimes select things I would never choose for myself, and more times than not, I end up loving the new look!

3. **Rock a new accessory.** I discovered this trick on bad hair days. I'd throw on a cute headband, a scarf, and some hoop earrings and receive tons of compliments! A fun handbag can also pull a look together.

4. **Give heels a chance.** In a world of comfortable sandals, flats, and tennis shoes, we can forget what a pair of heels can do. Pairing heels with jeans can dress up an everyday look. Or wear them with a dress for an upscale evening look. Just remember to practice before you go out, or you could end up drawing attention yourself for a different reason!

5. **Hit "refresh" on your normal makeup routine.** We all have our favorite cosmetics (I've used the same brand of blush forever). But an easy way to change up your look is to pick a new shade or try a new makeup technique. My YouTube channel is full of great makeup tutorials to get you started!

CHAPTER 5

LET'S TALK BEAUTY

Feeling beautiful has nothing to do with what you look like. I promise.

—EMMA WATSON

The day of my senior prom did not start out well. I was desperate to look great for my very last high school dance, so, for the first time ever, I went to a salon to get my hair done. But when I looked in the mirror at the end of the appointment, I didn't like the slightly messy updo I saw. The look wasn't *me*, and I was certain it was a total disaster.

For the rest of the day, I was stressed out. My mom tried to console me, but that only seemed to make matters worse. This was my senior prom, and I wanted to look good! Finally, I slipped into my polka-dot prom dress that flared at the bottom. A perfect fit! Then, as I started applying my makeup, I began to see a transformation. Suddenly, I thought, *My hair isn't that bad; in fact, I actually like it!* In the end, the look flowed together, I felt beautiful, and I had a wonderful evening at prom.

The answer to the question of what makes a woman feel beautiful is a complicated one. Can you remember the first time you truly felt beautiful? Maybe it was when you dressed up for a special event. Maybe you received a compliment about how you looked that stuck with you. Or maybe you have a special outfit that makes you feel beautiful.

While I was doing research for this book, I googled the question, "How can a woman feel beautiful?" And you know what—the Internet came up with almost zero results for that phrase. Instead, it replaced my

BEAUTIFUL WOMEN

Make a list of the most beautiful women you know. What makes them beautiful to you?

_____

_____

_____

Here are a few on my list:

My mom: My mom has a sweet nature, and her care for each of her kids inspires me. I want to be a mom like that someday. The way she loves unconditionally and supports each member of my family makes her beautiful to me.

My friend Charis: While all of my friends are beautiful, my friend Charis has especially inspired me. Her dramatic makeup looks are matched only by her spunky and passionate personality. She also ties everything she does back to Christ. Her bold, others-centered focus makes me want to live more selflessly and in the moment.

My sister: My sister, Kylie, has an amazing work ethic. She is diligent and dedicated, and the girl knows how to get results! Beautiful inside and out, she inspires me to put 100 percent into everything I do.

Who's on your list? I'm guessing the most beautiful women you've known don't necessarily look like supermodels. Remember that others feel this way about you too! Outward beauty has its place, but beauty that emanates from within makes a lasting impression on others.

search with, "How can a woman *look* beautiful?" There were thousands of results for that question!

The thing is, there's a big difference between *looking* beautiful and *feeling* beautiful. Some very attractive women do not feel beautiful. On the flip side, some women who look fairly average do feel beautiful. So what makes the difference? In this chapter, I hope to get to the bottom of that question.

THE POWER OF BEAUTY

When I first started my YouTube channel, my passion for what I was doing came from the amazing beauty videos I was seeing on the Internet. I watched tutorials by Michelle Phan and others, and I was amazed by how creative and artistic they were with their makeup. Their talent and the beauty they created inspired me to try new things, and to discover my own sense of style and self-presentation.

Over time, as I experimented with lots of beauty techniques, I became passionate about helping other girls discover their own individual beauty the way I had. I wanted those who followed my channel to know that it's okay to take inspiration from others. There's not an original statement out there in the world, and there's not an original makeup technique or outfit either; everyone's taking their inspiration from others. That's part of what YouTube is all about—sharing inspiration and helping each other by putting great ideas out there.

Because I believe collaboration is a major bonus of social media, a lot of my videos are about taking a trend and putting my own spin on it. I start with a beauty trend I like and then add my own preferences and flair to it. Too complicated? I can create my own easy hack to get a similar look. Don't love the smudged black eyeliner? I don't have to wear it that way. I can experiment with white and green eyeliner because I like the way it makes *my* eyes look.

To me, beauty is about fun and freedom. And there is a lot of freedom when you realize that you don't have to be 100 percent original (because that's not even possible!), but you can still be totally you. Pulling in ideas

from others adds more beauty to the overall picture, but you also don't have to do what everyone else is doing.

I follow a lot of beauty vloggers on Instagram, and I find inspiration from their styles every day. Sometimes a picture they post prompts me to try out a new look or expand on my own style. My hope is that when I post a video, my subscribers are inspired in a similar way and use what I offer as a springboard for expressing themselves in ways that only they can.

Many of us want to be original—we don't want to look exactly like everyone else. And as you play around with your hair, makeup, and clothes, you can create your own takes on beauty and put together looks that no one else can pull off in the same way. No one has the exact same face as you. No one has the exact same body as you, the same hair color, or even the same hands or feet! I give beauty advice to help my subscribers discover the ways God has made them beautiful and unique. As you put your own spin on style, you make a statement that there is no one else exactly like you.

BEAUTY BREAKDOWN

In the last chapter, I talked a lot about inner beauty and focusing on God and his opinion. So you may be wondering where fashion, style, and makeup fit in. Genesis tells us that God created humans in his image. Before sin came into the picture, Adam and Eve walked in the garden with God and talked to him every day. It must have been amazing to be the very first humans, living without sin in the world. The Bible says that they were naked and felt no shame.

But when Adam and Eve sinned, the *very first* thing that happened was they realized they were naked, and they sewed fig leaves together to make coverings for themselves (Genesis 3:7). After they sinned, their immediate instinct was to cover up. They felt ashamed. And I think we still feel remnants of this shame today.

I used to be unable to leave the house without wearing makeup. I was embarrassed due to my acne and didn't want anyone to see my "naked" face. I think the reason many of us spend hours in front of the mirror, trying to make our hair and makeup look perfect, goes back to that feeling Eve experienced when she realized her imperfection.

So what is the key to feeling beautiful? First Peter 3:3–4 says, "Your beauty should not come from outward adornment, such as elaborate hairstyles and the wearing of gold jewelry or fine clothes. Rather, it should be that of your inner self, the unfading beauty of a gentle and quiet spirit, which is of great worth in God's sight."

Our inner beauty is of *great worth* to God. It also lasts—unlike outward beauty, which can change or fade. Qualities that come from the inside, such as kindness, gentleness, and self-control, are the things that will last throughout our lives. So does this mean that we should never put effort into our outward appearance? I don't think so, and here's why.

As I've talked to hundreds of young women and listened to their stories, I've realized that looking good on the outside can totally change how you feel on the inside. Looking great gives you confidence and even changes how you interact with others. When a woman doesn't feel like she looks beautiful, it impacts every aspect of her life.

Not long ago, I watched this cool video about a hairdresser named Josh who gives haircuts to homeless people in London. He carries his tools with him, and when he meets a homeless person, he offers to give them a haircut. With permission, he posts his amazing before-and-after photos to his Instagram account, in the hopes of inspiring others to care about people living on the streets. You can see a dramatic difference in the expressions of his clients before and after they receive the haircuts. Josh has seen firsthand how a haircut can boost the confidence of people who haven't been able to take care of themselves for a while.

A makeover can transform how someone feels on the inside, which is one of the reasons I love what I do! I know I feel the most confident when I'm wearing a dress and my hair is curled. I'm more outgoing and comfortable around people, and I want to take pictures more often. For others they may feel most beautiful in a T-shirt and sweatpants. Everyone's sense of style is a little different, but most people feel more confident when they put effort into their appearance.

One thing I love to do is offer advice on dressing well, having great skin and hair, and finding your own makeup style. So let's break down this whole beauty thing.

CLOTHES

Clothes have been a thing since . . . well, since Adam and Eve left the garden of Eden and they covered themselves with fig leaves. But God made them better clothes. Genesis 3:21 says, "The Lord God made garments of skin for Adam and his wife and clothed them." *God clothed them.* This is powerful to me, because it tells me that our clothing matters to God. Here are three things clothing should do for you:

> **Cover your body.** This one is kind of a no-brainer. The main point of clothes is to cover our bodies. Clothes keep us warm in the winter. They help us look the part for certain activities, such as school, sports, or a job. There's nothing wrong with wearing a cute swimsuit to the beach or rocking shorts in the summer, but I always encourage people to think about dressing modestly.

That doesn't mean covering up from head to toe or wearing unflattering clothes—it means dressing in a way that makes you feel comfortable and appropriate for the situation at hand. Certain clothing styles aren't off-limits to Christians, but modesty should definitely influence all areas of our life, including the clothes we wear.

Magnify inner beauty. As I mentioned earlier, a beautiful spirit is what makes a woman truly beautiful. But the clothes we choose to wear can either emphasize or downplay what's on the inside. When I was in elementary school, I was kind of a tomboy, and my favorite ensemble was a pair of basketball shorts and a T-shirt. Then, in middle school, I noticed other girls dressing up. So I started wearing a dress now and then.

As I said earlier, for me, wearing a dress makes me feel feminine and self-assured. Other women may feel beautiful in jeans and a button-up shirt, or leggings and boots. It's all about what makes you feel amazing. And when you wear clothing that makes you feel confident, it helps you more accurately reflect the person God created you to be. In fact, once I started paying more attention to dressing appropriately for different occasions, I began to notice inner qualities God had put in me, such as the ability to reach out to others. I saw that the outfits I chose to wear could be an outward manifestation of who I was becoming on the inside. **Express individuality.** Think about your favorite outfit of all time. What makes you feel so amazing when you wear it? I love wearing a red dress. There's something magical about red to me; it's elegant, classy, and goes great with every skin tone.

One of the things I love about clothes is the many different ways I can express myself, using color, style, and accessories. There are a million different options! And no single outfit looks the same on each person, because we all look different. Everyone also has different fashion preferences: some people love a flannel and others love high heels. But even if you prefer one over the other, that doesn't mean you ever have to be limited to just one kind of style. Play around and find what works best for you.

So now that you know what clothes should help you do, how can you pick the right ones for you? Here are a few things to consider:

Fit. One of the most common mistakes people make when it comes to clothes is wearing things that don't fit correctly. Whether too big, too revealing, or too tight, there are a lot of ways clothes can go wrong. My advice is don't settle for clothes that don't fit correctly. Because I have a small waist and bigger hips, I've only found one store where the jeans fit me right. Don't be afraid to keep looking for a particular item, or to ask a trusted sales associate if something looks good on you.

Price. Many people in our age group are on a budget. While certain designer brands may be popular, I've found that expensive brands aren't necessarily the garments that look the best on me, and they definitely aren't good for my wallet. I check out the clothes at ordinary department stores and sometimes score big deals on outfits that look better on me than the designer brands.

You can also shop discount stores that sell brand-name clothes at a fraction of the price, or shop your favorite stores off-season. Not long ago, I was looking for summer clothes during the winter for a warm-weather vacation, and I was able to stock up on swimsuits and T-shirts at awesome deals.

Outside perspective. Have you ever loved an outfit and then seen a picture of yourself wearing it and thought, *That looks terrible on me. Why didn't someone tell me?!* Getting advice from others who you know will be honest—whether a friend, family member, or sales associate—can be a great way to find clothes that look great on you. Not sure if that skirt is flattering or frumpy? Ask your favorite shopping buddy. Not sure you can pull off the latest clothing trend? Ask a sales associate if there's a current look that might suit you better. Follow style accounts on Instagram or search Pinterest for outfit ideas for body types similar to your own.

SKIN

Your skin is the foundation of your look. It's the first thing people see when they meet you and when you have a conversation. Many people our age deal with acne, which can put a real damper on confidence. And while some will only get the occasional zit, others will struggle more significantly with their skin.

One friend who experienced severe acne during high school and into college described it this way: "No matter how clean I kept my face or how strict my diet was, my skin did not improve. I used vitamins and creams. I steamed, scrubbed, exfoliated. But nothing seemed to make a difference."

How did she get through it? "I realized that what was truly important about me was my relationship with God, not perfect skin," she says. "Regardless of my own opinion on my looks, God desired to use me to reach out to others. And that required looking them in the face—without shame—and being a reflection of the One who filled me with hope and life. After all, he created me with my flawed-skin genes. As much angst as it had caused me, there has been a purpose in it."

Whether you struggle with acne, like I did, or you've never had to wash your face a day in your life, there are a few basic rules that can help you get the best results for your skin.

Wear sunscreen. I use a daily moisturizer and a foundation that both have sunscreen. This is an easy way to protect your skin from daily sun exposure that can age your skin prematurely.

Keep it simple. Some skincare lines include a crazy number of products to put on your face. Most dermatologists will suggest keeping your routine simple and just using a cleanser, toner, and moisturizer. In addition, you may want to exfoliate and use a mask one to two times per week.

Work it. Choose a skincare routine that works for you. If you have more time in the morning, use products with active ingredients before you apply makeup and use a simpler regimen of cleansing and moisturizing before you go to bed. If you create a skincare routine that's easy to implement, you are more likely to be consistent.

Stick with it. When you try a new product, give it at least a month to work. Sometimes your skin may go through a detox process when you first start a new product, causing increased breakouts. If a product still isn't working for you after a month, it may be time to try something new. And if you have a severe reaction or a rash, definitely stop right away and talk to a doctor or dermatologist.

Regardless of how perfect or imperfect your skin is, remember that God finds you beautiful, flaws and all. I love this verse in 2 Corinthians 3:18, which says, "And we all, who with unveiled faces contemplate the Lord's glory, are being transformed into his image with ever-increasing glory, which comes from the Lord, who is the Spirit." What an amazing truth! Beauty may be only skin deep, but spiritual transformation changes your life.

HAIR

I've worn my hair in a similar style for most of my life. I like my hair long and versatile; I can curl it, straighten it, throw it into a ponytail, braid it, and a lot more. But I appreciate the short, sleek styles I see other women wearing.

Whatever your length, find a staple hairstyle that suits you. Most people don't want to put that much effort into their hair on a daily basis, so finding a hairstyle you can master is key. (For instance: If you can't work a round brush, don't get a style that's dependent on one.)

As you navigate the world of hair, here are a few things to consider:

Cut. To get a good cut, find pictures you like of styles in your length range—be it short, medium, or long—to show to your hairstylist. Your stylist can tell you if a style will work with your hair and the way it grows. Longer styles should generally be trimmed every eight to twelve weeks, while shorter styles may need to be maintained as often as every four weeks.

Color. Because I prefer to wear my hair long and layered, I've often experimented with color to spice up my look. Simple highlights can transform your whole style. In general, darker colors and lowlights work great in the fall and winter, while sunny highlights can brighten up your look in the summer. Then again, rules are

meant to be broken, so talk to your stylist about what looks good on you, and don't be afraid to try something new.

Texture. Every girl loves thick, luscious locks. While you can't change the basic texture of your hair, there are certain things you can do to make it appear thick and beautiful. Here are four ideas:

1. *Switch your part to the opposite side.* Shifting your part can give the hair around your roots a little lift, making your hair appear thicker at the top!
2. *Condition your hair before you shampoo it.* This technique can give your hair a more textured look.
3. *Use mousse.* Mousse works beautifully to give your hair a little extra lift and texture.
4. *Use dry shampoo.* Increased texture can completely change the appearance of your hair. Dry shampoo will give your roots an extra lift, even when your hair is clean!

Ease. A big part of finding the right style for you is deciding how much time and money you want to spend on maintenance. Are you a wash-and-go kind of girl? You may not want a style that you have to blow dry and style each morning. Do you only want to spend money on a hair cut every three to four months? Then a pixie cut or asymmetrical style is probably not for you. Love spending time on your hair and want to make it your signature look? Then go for a trendier style that requires more upkeep, but looks fresh and awesome!

The hairstyle you choose can flatter your face shape, enhance your style, and boost your confidence. Find a style that works for you and stick with it, or change it up regularly if that fits your personality! Your hair is as individual as you are, so take care of it and have fun.

MAKEUP

I love how makeup can totally transform a person's look in a way nothing else can. Experimenting with makeup was how I got my start on

YouTube, and I'm constantly keeping my eye on new makeup trends to update my own look.

That being said, I don't believe women have to wear makeup to look beautiful. In fact, in the past few years, some celebrities have made a big splash with their #nomakeup campaigns. Some women I know prefer to "go natural," and I think that's awesome. I've even gotten away from wearing makeup every day. If you're comfortable being makeup-free, more power to you!

But I also know the power makeup has to enhance a woman's natural beauty and boost her confidence. It can even out her skin tone, make her look less tired, emphasize her best features, and brighten up her overall countenance. There's nothing wrong with wearing makeup, especially once you learn how to do it right. If you're just getting started with makeup, here are a few fundamentals to consider:

Start small. There are a few basic cosmetics that can transform your look quickly. Some examples are concealer for under-eye circles and blemishes, foundation to even out skin tone, mascara to enhance lashes, blush to brighten cheeks, and lipstick to emphasize lips. You don't need every cosmetic. Start simple and add from there.

Accentuate eyes. I have dozens of videos showing eye makeup techniques, because there are so many things you can do to bring out your eyes. Here's some basic advice for applying eye makeup:

Primer. Start with a primer on your eyelids to avoid smudging.
Eye shadow. The easiest way to learn eye shadow techniques
is by using a color palette. First brush a base color (a color a
shade or two lighter than your skin tone) on the eyes up to
the brow bone, then apply a lid color (often a medium-brown

CREATE THESE GO-TO LOOKS

Every girl has her go-to looks. I used to scour fashion magazines for new
looks I could try. Here's how you can get three of my faves!

SUNDAY MORNING STYLE
How to get it:

Outfit: A-line patterned skirt, cami, denim-washed long-sleeve shirt tied
at the front, paired with some booties and socks.
Hair: Use a small bristle brush while you blow dry freshly washed hair for
a sleek look.
Makeup: Natural eyes with rosy cheeks and a pop of color on the lips.

LET'S WORK OUT!
How to get it:

Outfit: Leggings in a fun print, running shoes, tank top, and a jacket.
Hair: Pull hair up into a high ponytail with an elastic that holds your hair,
then put a fun scrunchie over it.
Makeup: None. Give your skin a breather!

DINNER WITH MY GIRLS
How to get it:

Outfit: Dark-wash skinny jeans, wedges, neutral top, and a jacket.
Hair: Use a curling iron with a 1/2-inch barrel to curl hair away from face,
creating face-framing layers.
Makeup: Dark, smoky eyes with a natural lip and contoured cheekbones.

color). Last, add the highlighter (the darkest color in your palette) toward the edge. Accentuate your eyes by choosing a shadow palette that's in the same color family as the hue of your eyes.

Eyeliner. To make your eyes appear bigger, use a white liner pencil on the inner rims and a darker liner on the outside. Or use a soft pencil and smudge to create a more natural line.

Mascara. Apply mascara near the roots and not the tips of your lashes to make your eyelashes look longer. To avoid eyelashes "clumping" together, wiggle the brush horizontally to separate them while applying mascara.

Play up lips. It's a general rule to either play up your eyes or your lips, not both at the same time. So if you do a dramatic eye, complement it with a nude or neutral lip. If you go with a more natural eye, try a pop of color with a red or fuchsia lip.

As you master makeup techniques, people will take notice. Women who wear little to no makeup on a daily basis can transform their look for a special occasion. And those that like to wear makeup daily can update their look with a small change. For me, makeup is about having fun and keeping my look fresh. Try experimenting with different aspects of makeup to find your perfect look.

FINDING YOUR (OUTWARD) BEAUTIFUL

As we talked about in the last chapter, beauty is as individual as people are. Just as your inner beauty looks different than mine, your outward beauty will also look different than mine. My hair may be my best feature, while your eyes or smile may be yours. Discovering what makes you feel beautiful, boosts your confidence, and allows you to shine your inward beauty to others is a process.

Trying new things is one great way to discover your own style. Let a friend do your makeup for a new look, or check out Pinterest for hairstyle ideas. Don't be afraid to experiment with different looks and be inspired by others.

Another way to find your beautiful is to focus on maximizing your best features. If you have a unique smile or your eyes tend to be very expressive, why not play it up? Try to *not* compare yourself to others. Comparison kills confidence, and we start to believe the lie that we aren't beautiful. When I choose to focus on who God has made me to be, realizing that he doesn't make mistakes, I silence the voice that tells me I'm not beautiful.

No matter how unhappy I am with something about my physical appearance, God made me that way for a reason. When I realize that truth, I can be thankful for who I am rather than be disappointed in who I'm not, allowing true beauty to shine forth as God transforms me from the inside out. And that's when I will truly *feel* beautiful.

XOXO,

Chels

Insider Beauty Tip:

TEN RIDICULOUSLY EASY BEAUTY HACKS

Achieving a stunning look is not as easy as it can appear on social media! Every girl needs a few simple tricks to look great. Here are ten of my all-time favorite beauty hacks:

1. For a perfect, natural blush effect, brush powder blush onto your cheeks before using foundation.
2. Apply Vaseline to the areas you typically put perfume before you spray. The Vaseline allows the perfume to hold its scent longer!
3. Rub an ice cube on your face before you apply makeup. This helps close the pores and reduce redness, resulting in more glowing skin.
4. To help nail polish go on smoother, put the bottle in the fridge for fifteen minutes before you apply it!
5. To reduce acne scars, mix a teaspoon of nutmeg and a tablespoon of honey into a paste and apply to the scarred area for thirty minutes. Rinse skin with warm water and pat dry. Repeat this treatment daily if you love it!
6. Rub or wrap a dryer sheet over your hairbrush before you use it to get rid of static in your hair. This simple trick really works!
7. Use nail polish remover to clean the stains off of the white parts of your Chucks, or any shoe with a white rubber sole.
8. Create your own makeup brush cleanser by mixing together one cup of water, one tablespoon of dish soap, and two tablespoons of vinegar.
9. To undo a bad fake tan from self-tanning lotion (trust me, I've been there), just scrub the area with baking soda to remove the color.
10. Create a detox bath by dropping in five to ten green tea bags while you're in the water. The antioxidants in the green tea will improve skin tone as you soak and relax your body.

CHAPTER 6

YOU NEED YOUR PEOPLE

Some people arrive and make such a beautiful impact on your life,
you can barely remember what life was like without them.

—ANNA TAYLOR

last year, I was going through a really hard time. I developed some health issues, had to drop out of college, and broke up with my boyfriend all within a month. All the changes left me feeling knocked down and disoriented.

On one particular day, a few weeks after I'd returned home to Illinois, I was feeling uncertain about some big decisions I needed to make, so I called up my friend, Kenzie, and asked if she could come over and talk. I was being a little selfish, because her long-distance boyfriend was in town for only a few days, but I really needed guidance.

The two of them dropped everything and came right over. They listened to what I was dealing with and some decisions I was planning to make. Then they posed some hard questions. They asked me what my goals were moving forward and what I had learned from some of the things I'd been going through. Then they asked how I could apply that knowledge to future circumstances and relationships. They also helped to clarify what I had already been thinking, and affirmed some tough decisions I needed to make.

That day, I really needed the support and wise counsel that could only come from a good friend. We all need friends we can depend on. God made us that way. Ecclesiastes 4:9–10 says, "Two are better than one, because they have a good return for their labor: If either of them falls down, one can help the other up. But pity anyone who falls and has no one to help them up."

All of my closest friendships have had that dynamic. We accomplish more together because my friend can be strong for me when I'm weak, and I can be strong for her when she's weak. Different friends can help you in different ways too. I have one friend whom I can laugh with for hours. And I have another friend who is super wise and always gives great advice. Each friend brightens my life in a different way.

When you encounter tough times, your true friends are the ones who are going to support you when you can't give much back. They'll be there when you're broken and you need them and you can't promise you'll be fun to be around. The best friends offer you wise advice, encourage you, and help you succeed.

FIVE TRAITS THAT MAKE FOR A GREAT BEST FRIEND

What do you look for in a friend? Here are the top five qualities that make my list:

1. **Compatibility:** You need to have things in common with your bestie. Maybe you have a similar sense of humor, a complementary taste in books or movies, or a shared fondness of shopping.

2. **Loyalty:** A friend who has your back and will support you through thick and thin is a must.

3. **Honesty:** A thriving friendship can't be fake. A great quality in a friendship is when you feel as if you can be completely truthful and open with one another.

4. **Sense of humor:** A best friend is someone you can laugh with. Even when you're having a tough day, you can find something funny that lightens the mood.

5. **Acceptance:** A best friend hears you out without jumping to conclusions. They accept you for who you are but also challenge you to be the best version of yourself.

THE SECRET TO MAKING FRIENDS

Finding great friends can be a challenge. I used to be a little clueless when it came to choosing the right kind of buddies, and I didn't start to develop deeper friendships until I was in high school. Something I discovered as I sought out friends I could depend on was that the number one factor in my success was *me*. I needed to *be* the kind of friend I was looking for—someone genuine who was kind no matter the circumstances, not quick to judge, and encouraging to those around me.

Once I started focusing on being the type of person others wanted to be friends with, a lot of amazing people started showing up in my life. Here are a few things to keep in mind as you seek out friendships:

> **Be the friend you want.** Find ways to exemplify the qualities you're looking for in a friend. For me, this includes kindness, dependability, loyalty, and humor. As you become a better friend, you will attract the type of friends you want. Don't think about what you might get out of a friendship, but choose to be the one who gives first—then see what happens.
>
> **Choose wisely.** Not everyone's intentions are good, so you have to choose friends carefully. The Bible tells us that bad company corrupts good character (1 Corinthians 15:33), and I've definitely experienced that. Like it or not, you become similar to the people you hang out with. If you don't want to get dragged down by poor choices, choose friends who will encourage you to live in a wise and healthy way.
>
> **Branch out.** I hear a lot of people complain that they can't find a good friend—especially a friend who is a good influence—at school. If this is you, try getting involved in groups outside of school hours, such as recreational sports leagues, community theater, or afterschool activities or clubs. You'll meet people who share your interests and possibly make a new friend in the process.
>
> **Find friends with faith.** One thing I recently learned is that when you have Christ in common, you'll always have a friend. Even if

there's a language barrier, an age difference, or you have opposite personalities, shared faith opens the door for friendship.

Don't give up. Finding even one good friend can be a difficult process. There may be times where you don't have a good buddy to call your own. During that lonely season, remember that Jesus is always there. As you depend on God, he will help you to grow and give you empathy for others who may be in need of a friend.

Also, don't limit yourself to friends your own age. Seek out someone older to provide some greater perspective, or spend more time with a sibling or an elderly friend or neighbor. Friends come in many different varieties, so don't be too quick to rule someone out.

THE FAMILY FACTOR

In some of my lonelier moments, my family has been my lifeline. Last fall, when I came back from college feeling weak and defeated, my family gathered around me and helped me get my footing back. My mom and I spent hours together, and my dad took care of all kinds of little details to lighten my load.

My family has its problems and hard moments, and just like any other family we don't always get along. But we're always there for each other no matter the circumstances. For example, my siblings are very different from me. Kylie is athletic, self-disciplined, and really good at school. Chandler loves playing video games but is also super funny with a sweet side. Even though each member of my family is different from the others, we know we can depend on one another. When one person in your family is going through something, you all go through it together.

Every family has its own dynamics. I am the oldest child. My siblings look up to me, so I'm careful about the example I'm setting. And when I mess up, I try to be honest about what happened. In a family, saying "I'm sorry" and "Will you forgive me?" is sometimes the best medicine. When I made some not-so-great choices my junior year, I was truthful

with my sister about mistakes I had made. I wanted Kylie to know that I wasn't perfect and that if she was ever struggling with something, she could always talk to me. That helped our relationship grow more than hiding the truth ever would.

My family is great at keeping me accountable to living the way I've said I want to live. But I've had to let them in. There was a time when I was more honest with my video camera, on YouTube, than I was with my own family. Now I focus on making my life more private on YouTube and more public to the people who care about me the most.

As grateful as I am for my support system, developing close family relationships is not always easy. You can get frustrated if you're making an effort, or have a goal for growing a relationship, and the other person isn't receptive. I don't know about you, but in my family, everyone gets busy doing his or her own thing. And sometimes it can feel like I'm under the same roof with these people I barely know.

When that happens, I try to keep showing my family members how much I appreciate them in ways they find meaningful. My mom loves to spend time together, watching a movie or scrapbooking, while my sister feels loved when I come out to support her at her tennis games. My dad appreciates verbal recognition for what he does for our family, and my brother loves to give and receive hugs. Finding what makes your family members feel loved and then doing those things on a regular basis can strengthen your relationships dramatically.

Maybe you're thinking, *That's nice for you, but my family is totally messed up.* Or, *You don't understand; I've lost someone.* Don't lose hope. Pray for the family members who are in your life, and seek out other people who may be able to fill in for family relationships you're missing. Keep your eyes open for someone at your church or school who could be a mentor and offer you guidance. Even a good friend can function like a family member. And don't forget about other believers; those in your church family can become like a real family that offers you support in life's ups and downs.

So focus on those who live within your four walls, but also the family of God. All it takes is showing up at church and looking for ways to get involved, whether that's attending a group for people your age, joining a small group, or volunteering to help with a ministry. Get to know the people who appear in your life, and be willing to lean on them for support and encouragement.

If you're away at college or in another situation where you don't see your family that often, find ways to stay in touch. With Skype, FaceTime, and dozens of instant messaging apps, checking in with your family members is easier than ever before. Texting multiple family members at once with a funny thing that happened in your day or a moment they would appreciate lets them know you're thinking of them and makes you feel closer.

The people who love you most share hundreds of memories with you and are going to be there for you when no one else is. Investing in those relationships is worth the effort.

HOW TO DRAMA-PROOF YOUR FRIENDSHIPS

When I took my senior trip to Panama Beach, Florida, I was excited to spend some time with friends one last time before we all graduated. But the trip lasted a week, and toward the end of it one of my friends and I were starting to get on each other's nerves. I'm not a sensitive person and can generally laugh when people make a joke about me or give me a hard time. But after several days of what felt like my friend picking on me, I'd had enough. First I withdrew and started being rude back. Finally, I told her, "Just leave me alone! I'm tired of being bullied!"

Drama in relationships can be really destructive. You can say and do things that cause real damage to the friendship. In the case of my friend, she didn't know she was hurting my feelings because I didn't tell her right when it happened. Instead of confronting my friend calmly and directly, I started venting to other friends about how frustrated I was. Eventually, my emotions boiled over and I blew up in anger.

We made up later and realized that we had simply been around each other for *way too long.* But I could have handled the situation better by being honest with my friend from the start. I should have talked to her privately rather than involving other people.

Proverbs 16:28 says, "A perverse person stirs up conflict, and a gossip separates close friends." We've probably all seen firsthand how those who stir up drama are destructive and how gossip ruins friendships. So how can we protect our friendships? Here are three pitfalls to avoid:

1. **Taking sides.** When your friends are having drama, sometimes you may feel stuck in the middle. Do your best not to take sides or be the middleman. Try to be objective, and encourage your

friends to talk to each other directly about the issue so they can resolve their differences more quickly.

2. **Gossip.** Let's face it, spreading rumors or talking negatively about people when they're not around is a major temptation. I know I've been guilty of doing it. So what's the big deal? Is it really that bad? The Bible mentions gossip eight times, and none of it's good.

   In James 3:5–6, James warns that although the tongue is a small part of the body, it can cause a lot of damage. He compares it to a small spark that starts a massive forest fire. Our words can quickly go out of control and be very destructive!

   Girls, our words matter. Not only should we avoid gossiping, we should shut it down when others start gossiping around us. Being bold enough to say, "We need to stop talking about this" can be really hard, but it's worth it and can totally diffuse damaging drama.

3. **Judgment.** When another person is rude or mean, it's easy to judge and think you know what's going on. But I try to remember that I'm not aware of the whole story. A person who is rude to me may be going through something terrible I know nothing about, and their behavior may have nothing to do with me. As Proverbs 11:12 says, "Whoever derides their neighbor has no sense, but the one who has understanding holds their tongue." I don't know about you, but I want to be a person who seeks to understand before judging.

BUILDING EACH OTHER UP

While lots of things can mess up friendships, there are a number of things that will help your friendships flourish. The secret is to replace the bad habits with good ones. Here are three ideas:

1. **Keep confidences.** One of the top qualities I look for in a

friend is someone who is trustworthy. Because I have such a public presence online, I have had to learn how to protect my friends and honor the things they share with me in private. A trustworthy friend who won't tell everyone else your business is a treasure.

2. **Challenge.** One of the best things about having a good friend is how the two of you can help one another to grow. Proverbs 27:17 describes it this way: "As iron sharpens iron, so one person sharpens another." You don't have to agree on everything— instead, you can help each other view life from a different perspective.

3. **Encourage.** We sometimes interact with other women in negative ways. We can be competitive, jealous, and catty. We can compare ourselves to others and tear them down to feel better about ourselves. In that kind of world, an encourager really stands out.

    I've tried to make it a habit to point out the strengths I see in

FIVE FRIENDS EVERY GIRL NEEDS

Friends come in many different varieties. Here are five pals I think every girl should have in her life:

1. **The Cheerleader.** This friend is an encourager. She celebrates your accomplishments and affirms your good decisions. The cheerleader sees the best in you and can reassure you when you're going through a hard time.

2. **The "Honest Abe."** This friend tells you the truth, even when it hurts. The Bible says that an honest answer is like a kiss on the lips (Proverbs 24:26). That means it's a really good thing! You need someone in your life who will give you an honest opinion and not just tell you what you want to hear.

3. **The Childhood Bestie.** This friend has known you *forever*. She knows the name of the hamster you had in first grade and your favorite music

other people. I once heard that if you notice something good in someone, you should tell them! A simple compliment, such as, "I really like that outfit on you," or, "You spoke so clearly during that presentation" can really build someone up. We all have different gifts and abilities, so we shouldn't be afraid to call out the good things we see in others.

JUST BE NICE

My high school yearbook had pages of "Senior Superlatives." These awards, which included "prettiest eyes" and "most athletic," were mostly based on talents or fun, inconsequential quirks. But one of the awards, "Nicest Seniors," was a little different. Everyone in the class agreed on the two people who should be chosen for this award because of their energy, enthusiasm, and positivity. They were the people who always had a smile on their face and a kind word for everyone.

from middle school. You and your childhood BFF may not always be best friends, but having a pal who grew up with you, and who shares your memories and inside jokes, is pretty amazing.

4. **The Mentor.** This friend is usually someone older and wiser. But she may be someone your age who's a little farther down the road than you are. My mentor, Charis, started out as a friend. Then I realized she was giving me all this amazing spiritual guidance, so I asked her to be my mentor. Having at least one friend like this can be extremely valuable.

5. **The Mood-Lifter.** This friend can make you feel better about life in the midst of a rainstorm without an umbrella. When life gets hard, you need this girl to lighten the mood and make you laugh. If you're having a bad day, chances are you'll feel a lot better after spending time with this ray of sunshine.

Maybe you've met that kind of people. Their positivity and kindness spreads like wildfire and seems to put everyone in a good mood. I'm not always good at it, but it really is easy to be nice to others . . . and you might even make a new friend!

FRIENDS FOR THE JOURNEY

When I was in eighth grade, God gave me an unlikely friend. I met Charis at the NYX Face Awards. A beauty vlogger like me, Charis had this amazing, magnetic personality. She loves Jesus and she wasn't afraid

to tell anyone about it! Charis is ten years older than me, but our shared faith and purpose in life bonded us immediately.

Even though she lived in Alaska and I lived in Illinois, we kept in touch after the competition, talking often about what God was doing in our lives. Sometimes we would pray together over the phone. We even went on a mission trip together!

Charis is an encourager, and has continued to find out what's happening in my life and give me solid advice. Our relationship isn't necessarily a best friend relationship—it's more of her encouraging me and showing me how to grow. She's a wise leader in my life, and I consider her friendship one of God's greatest gifts to me. And I hope, as she sees the influence she's having in my life, she is inspired to encourage even more young women.

Not every friendship will last a lifetime, and that's okay. Some people will come into your life for a little while and then fade out. Maybe you've experienced "growing apart" from someone you used to be really close with. Having different friends at different points in your life is natural. But sometimes you'll meet a friend you will have for a lifetime. These are friends for the journey.

Both "friends for a season" and "friends for the journey" are valuable. God uses them in different ways to help you to grow and shape you into the person he's transforming you to be. Some of the most beautiful experiences in life happen within the context of friendship.

Stay in the habit of making friends throughout your life. There's an old song that goes, "Make new friends, but keep the old. One is silver, the other is gold." Whether your friends are old or new, they are a treasure, and a person who has a true friend is very rich. Thank God for your friends and do your best to treat them well!

XOXO,

Chels

Insider Beauty Tip:

DIY PAMPER PARTY WITH A FRIEND

You don't have to go to an expensive spa to get in some pampering. Grab a friend, sister, or your mom, put on a movie, and pamper yourself with one of these easy treatments.

Perfect Pedis: Start by exfoliating feet using a sugar scrub. Apply cuticle oil to each toe and push back cuticles. Trim and file nails to your liking. Soak feet in a bowl of warm water for several minutes, and dry feet with a towel. Apply two coats of polish; you can also apply a top coat of clear polish to reduce chipping. Once nails are dry, moisturize feet and put on fuzzy socks or slippers.

Fabulous Facials: Use products you have on hand, such as a mask or peel, or try making this easy banana face mask recipe. (Bananas are packed with vitamins and nutrients that make it a super beauty fix.) In a small bowl, mix together 1/4 cup plain yogurt, 2 tbsp honey, and a smashed banana. Apply it to your face for about fifteen minutes. Rinse it off and enjoy your smooth skin.

Super Soft Hands: Mix together 1/4 cup + 1 tbsp of coconut oil, 1/2 cup raw or granulated sugar, and 1 tbsp honey. (For yummy smells, add five to six drops of essential oils like lemon, orange, or peppermint.) Massage mixture onto hands for two minutes. Rinse hands with lukewarm water and pat dry with a towel. (Store the extra scrub in a small plastic container or jar. It keeps up to a month.)

Enjoy your pamper party!

CHAPTER 7

DEALING WITH HATERS

Don't let people's compliments go to your head and don't let their criticisms go to your heart.

—LYSA TERKEURST

I think I must have the most wonderful subscribers in the world. When I was first getting started, they flooded the comments section of each video with praise and encouragement that has never really let up. They loyally voted me through to the final six in a national makeup competition. And as my YouTube channel has grown, they have shared their hearts with me and faithfully cheered me on. It's like I have this extra family online who has grown up with me.

I have been overwhelmed by the kindness, humor, and camaraderie I've experienced through my subscribers and the YouTube community. And to my subscribers and YouTube friends who are reading this— thank you! You have truly changed my life and made me a better person. There's no way I'd be doing what I'm doing without you. When I tell you online that *I love you*, I mean it with all of my heart!

While living my life in the public eye has definitely come with a ton of blessings and amazing opportunities, it has provided its share of drawbacks as well. With over a million people following my videos, not everyone is going to like what I do. Putting my life out there opens me up to scrutiny from people I've never even met. I've encountered viewers who criticize my appearance, my advice, my character, my life choices, and even my beliefs.

FIVE WAYS TO SPREAD POSITIVITY ONLINE

Social media can be an easy place to complain and lash out at people you disagree with. But I've seen beautiful acts of kindness online. Here are a few ways to spread the love online:

1. **Start an encouragement thread.** Create a post asking each person to write a compliment or encouraging word for the person who posted before her.

2. **Silence negativity instead of blocking it.** Instead of creating drama on Twitter by unfollowing people who post negative content, use the Mute button to get their negativity out of your feed. There are times you'll need to delete someone from your social media, but refrain from doing it over little annoyances.

Early on, I had to learn how to manage all the opinions—positive and negative—that were flying my way. I had to figure out how to cope when people criticized my work. When I first started my channel, I did a lot of costume tutorials, such as a Barbie look or a fairy princess look. I often took my inspiration from other beauty influencers and added my own spin on the looks. As a result, some people accused me of copying those other influencers and not having actual talent of my own.

The first few times I received mean and negative comments, it came as a shock, and I had a really hard time getting past those words. I took the negative comments to heart and would agonize over them for weeks. Even though I didn't feel like I had copied someone else's work, I let the criticism tear me down and make me feel bad about myself.

TYPES OF HATERS

You may remember that hit Taylor Swift song from a few years ago that talks about how haters are going to hate. Some people are going to dislike

3. **Make an encouragement sandwich.** This is a great way to offer constructive criticism. When you need to disagree or say something negative, start and end by saying something positive. An "encouragement sandwich" can help the person receive your critique more easily and know that you care.
4. **Start a happy hashtag challenge.** Post a picture promoting something you care about, and tag three friends to do the same! You could do a nature photo challenge, a friendship challenge, or a love-your-pet challenge.
5. **Create a Flipagram.** Use the Flipagram app to put together pictures of people you care about. Add a meaningful caption to share the love online!

you no matter what. Swift talks about people judging her life, and criticizing the things she does and even who she is. We've all been there! A part of life is encountering people who don't like you, or who don't seem to approve of what you do or who you are. Here are a few types of haters:

Frenemies. A "frenemy" is someone who claims to be your friend but consistently does things that are not in your best interest. In middle school, I had a friend like this. She caused drama at school (shunning me from my normal lunch table), had a birthday party where she invited all of our friends but me, and even sent me a text cussing me out after I insisted on sitting with my boyfriend at lunch, when she wanted to sit with him.

Shortly after that text, my parents made me quit spending time with those friends because it was turning into a bullying situation. Before that happened, my friendship with that girl completely stressed me out. I was hurt, but I was afraid that if I cut her out of my life, I'd lose the rest of my friends too. I constantly wondered what she and my other "friends" were saying about me when I wasn't around—because it seemed like everyone talked negatively about the others behind their backs.

Bullies. A bully is someone who is unkind, cruel, or aggressive toward someone who appears weaker than them. Those who bully use their power—whether that's physical strength, access to information, or popularity—to control or hurt others. Bullies repeat this behavior over a period of time, and these behaviors may include making threats, spreading rumors, attacking someone physically or verbally, or intentionally excluding someone from a group.

Bullying is a huge issue in our world, especially in schools. It can cause lasting emotional and psychological damage to both the person being bullied and the person doing the bullying. Many schools have created antibullying programs to try to decrease the damage caused by this behavior.

Cyberbullies. A cyberbully is someone who uses the same tactics as a bully, but uses electronic technology to act out his or her aggression. They may use text messaging or social media to harm others. Examples of cyberbullying include mean text messages, rumors posted on social media, and embarrassing pictures, videos, or websites shared with the world. Some cyberbullies even create fake profiles that perpetuate false information.

Cyberbullying is particularly bad because it means someone can be bullied 24/7, even when she is alone and few other people know about it. Also, communication distributed electronically can be difficult to trace or erase.

Gossips. We already talked a bit about gossip in the last chapter. Gossip divides friends, stirs up drama, hurts feelings, and spreads false information. A simple definition of gossip is discussing the personal details of another person's life or situation when you and the listener are neither part of the problem nor part of the solution.

When I made the decision to take a semester off from college—and began to open up about that on YouTube—I noticed some people speculating on my motives and discussing how I was just a privileged "princess" who couldn't handle the real world. It made me angry, because these people had no idea what I was going through or the many factors that had led to my decision.

Slanderers. A slanderer takes gossip to the next level, maliciously seeking to ruin someone's reputation through the spread of false rumors. Maybe you've been the target of a false rumor at school. A slanderer can do a lot of damage, and it can take a while to correct a false report and get your reputation back.

The types of people I described above—plus others who dislike us or actively seek to harm us—are referred to as enemies in the Bible. That's not a word we use a ton these days, outside of epic action movies or war references. But enemies do exist, and the Bible talks a lot about how we should treat them.

HOW TO TREAT PEOPLE

Before we talk about how we should respond to haters, I think it's helpful to think about how we should treat people in general. Someone once asked Jesus what God's greatest commandment was. This was his answer: "'Love the Lord your God with all your heart and with all your soul and with all your mind.' This is the first and greatest commandment. And the second is like it: 'Love your neighbor as yourself'" (Matthew 22:37–39).

Jesus could have picked one of the biggies, like "You shall not murder," or "You shall not steal," but he said the greatest commandment was love—love for God and love for your neighbor. And Jesus wasn't talking about the next-door neighbor who waters your plants when you're on vacation or brings you Christmas cookies; he was talking about *anyone*

you encounter who has been created in God's image. That's everyone.

I don't know about you, but that idea changes everything for me. The biggest thing God expects of me is to love him and love my fellow human. And you may think that *surely* God would let us off the hook when it comes to loving a truly horrible and heinous person, but that's not true. Listen to another shocking thing Jesus said: "You have heard that it was said, 'Love your neighbor and hate your enemy.' But I tell you, love your enemies and pray for those who persecute you, that you may be children of your Father in heaven" (Matthew 5:43–45).

It makes sense to love those who love us and hate those who hate us, right? But Jesus introduced this idea that our enemy is also our neighbor—a person we are called to love. Not only that; he tells us to *pray* for those who persecute us, because that identifies us as God's children.

Loving those who hurt us can be one of the hardest things to do. When someone hurts me, I have to choose to give grace, knowing that I can never know the full story of what's going on in that person's life and what hurts and pains she might be dealing with. Even when a person continues to cause pain that seems completely unwarranted, Jesus still tells me to forgive that person (Luke 17:4). That forgiveness can happen when I recognize that God has forgiven me for my wrong choices, and realize he loves that other person so much that he died for her! Who am I to hate, when Jesus so freely loves and forgives?

WHEN AN ENEMY ATTACKS

A few years ago, I published an article on my website about modesty. I talked about how, as a Christian, I want to glorify God through the clothes I wear and not draw undue attention to myself by dressing in ways that are overly revealing or provocative. I quickly found out this is a very controversial topic!

Another beauty influencer, who had a much larger following than me, tweeted about my article, saying, "I don't think anyone should be judged on how much skin she shows." She blew up in anger against me, and then a bunch of other people jumped on the bandwagon and started tweeting hurtful comments.

I personally messaged the young woman, explaining that I hadn't meant to offend her and that I was simply sharing my own perspective. But my words had hit a nerve, and it became clear that she wanted to remain fired up about it. I felt crushed by the firestorm of criticism that her tweet stirred up.

In the end, I had to accept that as much as I don't like offending others, sometimes people will be offended. And sometimes people will dislike me, misunderstand me, and say unfair things about me. For example, when I post videos relating to my faith, I occasionally get push-back from some of my subscribers, telling me why God isn't real or why I'm foolish to believe in the Bible. They threaten to unsubscribe or block my faith posts. But I figure if people dislike me for my faith in Christ, that is one of the best reasons to be disliked.

In those moments, I remember the words Jesus said to his disciples: "If the world hates you, keep in mind that it hated me first. If you belonged to the world, it would love you as its own. As it is, you do not belong to the world, but I have chosen you out of the world. That is why the world hates you" (John 15:18–19).

If people hate me as a result of my faith or the way I choose to live because I follow Christ, that's okay. Jesus even said it's normal! There is a lot of darkness in the world, and sometimes people just don't like the light. I've had to realize that on occasion the real thing offending them is God's truth, not me.

On the other hand, there can be legitimate reasons someone might dislike me. In fact, Christians get a bad name for being judgmental, legalistic, hypocritical, or holier-than-thou. And it's true that Christians can be all of these things. So when I am criticized, whether it's online or in person, I try to think about what was going on in my heart when I posted that video or said or did that thing someone is upset about.

Here's an example: After I got free of my toxic middle school friends and started spending time with true friends, I realized I had a gossiping problem that had followed me from those other relationships. One day I was talking negatively about someone, and a friend said, "Chelsea, you're

FIVE WAYS TO TURN CRITICISM INTO MOTIVATION

As I've experienced criticism in my life, I've found that although it can hurt, harsh words can also bring healthy change.

1. **Look for the nugget.** When someone criticizes you, don't immediately dismiss what they say. Instead, see if there's something you can take from it. When people accused me of copying other beauty influencers, I started making my videos and looks even more original, and the negative comments subsided.

2. **Channel your angst.** If someone's comment makes you feel bad about yourself, find a positive way to combat the emotional damage. When I was struggling with criticism after leaving college, I started a regular running routine. The running gave me time to clear my head and realize that other people's opinions of me didn't really matter.

3. **Try something new.** Sometimes in the midst of hurt or rejection, you just want a "reset button." One time when I was feeling down, I tried longboarding. Learning something new can make you feel like a different person and help you to shake off discouragement.

4. **Don't hate the hater.** Realize that your battle is not with another human being. Most people's intentions aren't cruel, especially if that person cares about you. Try to assume the best in the people who criticize you, and don't let any one person derail you from the good you could be doing.

5. **Keep moving forward.** When I see negative comments, I'm tempted to linger on those harmful messages. It can be hard to move on from them. But I make myself go forward. Something is true about every one of my videos: some people will love it and some people won't. I try to allow criticism to drive me to be even better the next time.

being really rude right now." At first I was taken aback, but I quickly realized she was right. I was being rude!

Not all criticism is bad. Being criticized can cause us to examine our hearts and find ways God is asking us to change. Proverbs 27:6 says, "Wounds from a friend can be trusted, but an enemy multiplies kisses." My former friends said plenty of nice things to my face, but then tore me down behind my back. My new friends were the opposite; they cared about me enough to call me out when I was behaving badly and to challenge me to do better. And as I learned more about how God wanted me to treat others, I started to do the same for them.

At times, it can be difficult to tell the fake friends from the real ones. Your mom may tell you something you don't want to hear, such as, "I don't like that guy you're dating," and you simply want to pass it off as her being negative or unsupportive. Or maybe a friend mentions that you seem to be acting a little stuck up lately, and you assume she's just jealous. Remember that not all criticism should be "shaken off" as Ms. Swift prescribes. Handling legitimate critique in the right way can be a great learning experience.

DEALING WITH CRITICISM

So how can you handle criticism in a healthy way? Here are a few things I've learned through various experiences:

Consider the source. When I first started getting negative comments on my YouTube videos, I took them to heart and got really down on myself. But I had to remember that these comments were coming from people behind a screen who knew next to nothing about my life. In those cases, it was easier to shake off the criticism and move on. If the person offering critique was a friend or family member, though, I could consider their opinion more deeply because they knew me and were qualified to speak into my life.

Talk to somebody you trust. When hurtful comments come my way, I like to talk it through with a trusted friend or family member. People who know me well can offer perspective and help me look past the sting of criticism and see the truth. The point isn't to rant and complain but to seek out helpful advice and view something from an outside angle. Other times you just need someone who will let you be sad and eat ice cream with you when you've been hurt.

Don't engage. In the situation where I was attacked for my article about modesty, I tried to make things right by going directly to the person who took issue with it. When that didn't work (and actually seemed to make matters worse), I decided the best thing to do was ignore the storm of criticism until it went away.

If people don't want to hear what you have to say—or don't like you—you can end up wasting time and energy trying to explain yourself and bring them around to the truth. Pick your battles, and accept that there will be people who simply won't see things your way.

Focus on the positive. When I get negative comments on a YouTube video, I try to remember all of the positive comments I receive. Once when I posted a photo to Instagram that was a close-up of my face, people started talking about how I had no upper lip. At first I was really hurt by the comments, especially since they were about a physical characteristic I had no control over! I needed to remember that even though that part of me didn't satisfy some people's ideal of beauty, I *am* beautiful in my own ways.

The truth is, people can always find something about you that isn't perfect. And you may be unfortunate enough to hear them say it. In those moments, remember all of the positive things about yourself and choose to focus on those attributes. That's easier said than done, but I've found doing that really lifts the weight of criticism.

Khoudia Diop, a Senegalese model, grew up being bullied about her very dark skin. But once she hit the modeling scene at age seventeen, it was her unique skin tone that led to her stunning success. Now she tells young women, "If you're lucky enough to be different, don't ever change." As Khoudia's story shows, people sometimes let what they see on the outside lead them to say hurtful things. But God created every single person in his image, and things we're led to believe are physical flaws simply aren't. That is the truth that will bring us together and allow us to see beauty in each other's differences.

Let it go. Over time, I've learned to not take the criticism so personally. Not long ago, I posted a video that included my fitness routine and some of my health habits. A vegan extremist made a whole video in response to my video, picking apart my advice and saying I was trying to kill my subscribers! I actually found it funny and knew I had grown a lot in this area. When criticism seems to come out of left field, sometimes making light of it and letting it go is the best tactic.

GETTING FREE FROM HATERS

Haters may be a part of life, but we don't have to let them ruin ours.

The best thing to do when people wrong us is to treat them with love and forgive their wrongs just like God would. That's not always easy to do. Sometimes it's exhausting to feel like you always have to be the "bigger person," or the one who overlooks the bad behavior of others.

At times when I've tried to repair a relationship with someone who has wronged me, the person doesn't seem to understand or appreciate what I'm doing. They may even act like I'm weird for trying to move past our disagreement. But in those moments, I know I'm following Jesus' instructions to love my enemy, and that's all that really matters.

Even when it seems like those efforts aren't making a difference, who can say that I haven't planted a seed in someone's life that may grow into something beautiful later? Down the road, that person may think back on what happened and choose a better path going forward.

We're all going to encounter haters in our lives, and we're all going to receive criticism at times. The best thing we can do is to act out of love and show kindness, even when doing so feels impossible. All things are possible with God. Don't join the haters. Love them.

XOXO,

Chels

Insider Beauty Tip:

PLAYING UP YOUR BEAUTY STRENGTHS

Because of the industry I'm part of, people sometimes say hurtful things about my appearance. I rise above the critiques by focusing on the things that make me unique. Whether you receive compliments on your gorgeous brown eyes or lusciously curly hair, play to your strengths, girl!

Eyes: Go online to identify your eye shape. Then learn techniques for different looks that work best with the shape of your eyes. You'll be surprised by the illusions you can create with eye makeup, such as making your eyes look bigger or making their color pop!

Lips: Try lining your lips and filling them in with a darker color than you would usually go for. Emphasizing the shape of your lips can add character to your face and give you increased confidence.

Body shape: Just about everyone looks nice in a dress. Research the best style of dress for your body type. Curvier women look great in something semifitted, such as a wrap dress. If you have short legs and a long torso, a simple A-line dress may suit you best. Have a bit of a tummy? Empire styles make your midsection fade away. Choose a dress that fits your frame, and plan a night out with your girls. Instant confidence booster!

Hair: To emphasize great hair, try something new. If you typically wear a ponytail, wear your hair down in loose curls. If you always wear your hair down, try a fancy "down-

do," such as two braids that go from either side of the crown of your head and connect in the back. (Pinterest offers tons of creative ideas!) Changing up your hair can add interest to your look.

Skin: Have glowing skin? Opt for light coverage foundation or BB cream to allow your flawless skin to show through. Want to create a glamorous look? Learn to contour! This enhances any face shape, as you work with your natural structure. You can find lots of how-to instructional videos online!

CHAPTER 8

BOYS, RELATIONSHIPS, AND ROMANCE

The right relationship won't distract you from God. It will bring you closer to him.

—JASON EVERT

I had my first boyfriend in sixth grade. He was cute and blond, with a sideswept Justin Bieber haircut. Our favorite thing to do together was go to the Great Skate on a Friday night to rollerblade and hang out with friends. The rink was always packed with middle school kids sporting Aéropostale fashions and body spray. We would zip around the rink to hits like "I Gotta Feeling" and "Party in the U.S.A."

There wasn't a lot to romantic relationships at that age. You basically had a special friend at school, and if the relationship was really epic, you might *kiss* at some point. And so it happened that one night at the Great Skate, about a month after we'd been dating, my boyfriend and

I found ourselves sitting on a bench surrounded by our friends, who began chanting, "Kiss, kiss, kiss!"

We complied, giving the fastest peck the world has ever known. My memories of that night are so vivid—who was there, what I was wear-

ing. Despite that sweet moment, our sixth-grade puppy love didn't last. But we'll always have the Great Skate and that memorable first kiss!

In the years since my first boyfriend, I've learned a lot about dating and romance. Some of the lessons have been hard. Others have been funny. Still others have given me insight on how to have godly relationships and even think ahead to marriage someday.

THE CONFUSING WORLD OF DATING

Sometimes I wish dating would have stayed as simple as it was in sixth grade. In my small town, middle school dating was fun, innocent, and a community event! As I've gotten older, however, relationships have definitely become more complicated.

One young adult blogger put it this way:

"I often wonder what happened to old-fashioned dating—dating in the sense of being able to spend time with a person but not be 'exclusive,' not be 'complicated,' not be 'together,' but to just be in one another's company. Instead, dating has evolved into a pressure-filled, semi-confusing, yet rewarding endeavor" (Beth Leipholtz, "5 Reasons 'Dating' as a Millenial Is Traumatic, Confusing and Fantastic," *Huffington Post,* July 16, 2014).

The reasons for the pressure and confusion surrounding romantic relationships are many, but experts have highlighted that constant communication (texting), social media, online dating sites, and a "hook-up culture" are a few things that make dating today tricky to navigate. And while having a romantic relationship can be hard enough, when you add to the mix being a Christian—and attempting to date in a way that pleases God—it can seem nearly impossible! You find yourself asking questions like:

Should I date someone?
What should my reasons for dating be?
What if no one wants to date me?
What does a healthy relationship look like?
Is it okay to date in the same way my friends do?
How far can I go physically in a relationship and still be okay with God?

These are really important questions, and ones that I've had to answer for myself over the years. And I certainly haven't figured everything out. But before we really dive into answering these and other questions, here are a few important things to consider about romantic relationships:

God established romance. When you hear people mention the boundaries God puts on relationships (we'll talk more about that later), you can get the impression he's a big killjoy when it comes to love and romance. But that's just not true. He designed relationships! He is the source of all love, including romantic love. And when we love others the way he intended, romantic love can be one of the most beautiful things in this life.

Romantic love isn't a new concept, either. When God created Adam, he said that it was not good for the man to be alone. He needed a partner, and God provided Eve to be Adam's wife. God is a romantic, y'all! Throughout the Bible, you see love stories: Jacob and Rachel; Ruth and Boaz; Joseph and Mary. God delights in a good love story!

Timing is key. One of the most epic love stories in the Bible is Song of Songs. Written by a great king named Solomon, the book tells the story of the king meeting a beautiful young woman, falling in love with her, and eventually marrying her. It's the kind of story that makes a girl weak in the knees. We all long to be loved, cherished, and sought after like the king's beloved.

Throughout the book, a key phrase keeps popping up: "Do not arouse or awaken love until it so desires" (Song of Songs 2:7, 3:5, and 8:4). It means that we shouldn't force love to happen until the right time. That is really hard to do. We live in a world that tells us romance is basically the meaning of life! We're encouraged to seek it out. I remember feeling a lot of pressure in high school to be dating someone or to have a boyfriend. But for a lot of people, high school may not be the right time to fall in love naturally. More on that later!

You can be a Christian and date. The world's views on dating—what is normal and allowable—can go directly against the principles found in the Bible. (For example, the right timing for sex.) Because of this, people have been debating for decades if Christians can date in a godly way. Here's what I think: You can do just about anything in a godly way or an ungodly way. For instance, it's easy to cheat in school, and cheating is pretty widespread. But it's also very possible to go through school, and even graduate, without cheating.

Same goes for dating relationships. Are there pitfalls and temptations you have to watch out for when you're dating someone? Absolutely. Is it possible to date with integrity and purity? Yes!

Romantic relationships have purpose. Like my sixth-grade dating experience illustrates, not every relationship is going to end in happily ever after. But that doesn't mean that each relationship is without a purpose. These days, as I'm approaching my twenties, I realize that any guy I date could end up being my husband, so exploring that possibility will probably be a main purpose of my relationships.

TEN GREAT DATE IDEAS

A fancy evening out can be fun, but dates don't have to be extravagant or expensive to be memorable. Here are ten of my favorites:

1. **Picnic in the park.** Pack a picnic lunch where each of you contributes some of your favorite foods. Spread out a blanket and enjoy a scenic spot to eat and talk.

2. **Dance like no one's watching.** Go to an empty parking lot (in a safe location), let music play out your car windows, and dance.

3. **Video stars.** Make a music video together (using an app like Video Star). Make different cuts of a song and edit until you produce the perfect video.

4. **Dress-up date.** Get dressed up and go for dinner at your favorite restaurant, even if it's not a "fancy" place. (Who says homecoming or prom has to be the only time you dress up for a date?)

5. **On holiday.** Holidays provide all kinds of special events that make for fun dates. Go see fireworks on the Fourth of July, check out Christmas lights at the zoo, or go to a St. Paddy's Day parade.

6. **Serve.** Sign up to serve at your church, or collect donations for a worthy organization. Not only can you have fun working toward a cause, you can see more of your boyfriend's heart for service.

7. **I spy.** Many towns have escape rooms, where you (and a group of friends) can get locked in a room together and have to solve a mystery. Get in touch with your inner spy by using your wits and ingenuity to solve puzzles and escape before time runs out!

8. **School spirit.** Go to a football game, band concert, or school play. You can support your school and have a fun night out at the same time!

9. **Game on.** If you like a little competition, gather up some of your favorite board games (or try a new one!) and some tasty snacks. Host a group of friends or invite your family members to join in for a night of friendly rivalry!

10. **Get moving.** Walking, running, biking, and playing tennis are all great ways to get active and have fun. These activities allow time for conversation while also helping you stay in shape.

However, sometimes the purpose of a relationship may be for you to build that other person up, or to show you more about yourself and the type of person who might be right for you long term. Realizing that relationships have purpose and aren't just for fun (although they can be a lot of fun!) is important, because it helps you to make the most of every relationship God brings into your life.

HOW NOT TO DATE

I've made mistakes in my dating life, and I've learned things too. Sometimes a guy who makes a great friend doesn't make a great boyfriend. Dating a "bad boy" isn't all it's cracked up to be. Trying to change someone won't always work—in fact, instead of making someone else better, you might find yourself making bad decisions because of a bad influence.

I know firsthand how a romantic relationship can put tension on relationships with your family, your friends, and even with God. I once dated a guy who wasn't good for me. He was a smart, interesting person, and even though we didn't share the same beliefs or even all of the same values, we had a connection. But being with him led me to make choices I knew I shouldn't make—like sneaking around and dating him even though my parents didn't approve. Eventually, I realized I needed to step away from the situation and find someone who was a better match. I'm so glad I did.

After that, I realized I didn't want to date guys who didn't share my faith. This was a personal decision I knew was right for me—Jesus was the most important relationship in my life, and I wanted to find someone who felt the same way. Going forward, I decided to date guys who agreed with me on the big stuff, like faith and family. But we didn't have to agree on everything. In fact, one of the best parts of dating is learning from and growing with that other person!

Even if you're not a Christian, you can be thoughtful about who you date. Just as you choose good friends, choose guys to date who share your values, respect you, are kind, and who make you a better person.

HOW TO GET THE MOST OUT OF DATING

Now that you've learned from me how *not* to date, let's talk about how *to* date. Dating is one of my favorite things in the world. There's nothing like the feeling of dressing up and holding a guy's hand for a special event or night on the town. Then again, doing something casual together, like riding bikes or having a picnic in the park, can be equally fun! I love how God made men and women so different, and how our varying perspectives on life can help us learn and grow.

After I was in that bad relationship, I experienced a really good one. My next boyfriend loved God and showed me respect. Being in a healthy relationship was refreshing. My boyfriend and I attended Bible study and youth group together and could talk about what we were learning. We made it a priority to put Christ at the center of our relationship. And, boy, did that make a difference!

The dating thing was a lot easier when we had faith in common, but it still took some work. Here are a few things I learned are important to having a healthy relationship:

Wisdom. A big factor in dating well is wisdom. Being in a relationship requires a lot of decisions—big and small. And wisdom helps you make the right ones. Listen to what Proverbs says about it: "Blessed are those who find wisdom, those who gain understanding, for she is more profitable than silver and yields better returns than gold . . . She is a tree of life to those who take hold of her; those who hold her fast will be blessed" (3:13–14, 18).

I don't know about you, but I want to get in on that! And we can. We simply have to ask God for wisdom and he'll give it to us generously! No strings attached.

Purity. God delights to see purity in our lives. In romantic relationships, staying pure—in our thoughts and actions—can be a challenge. So how do we do it? Psalm 119:9 says, "How can a young person stay on the path of purity? By living according to your word."

My greatest resource for knowing how to live has been the Bible. It reminds me to avoid situations where I am tempted to do something I know is wrong. It tells me to protect my heart, which

WHAT I LOOK FOR IN A GUY

As you may have figured out, I love lists! A few years ago, I decided to write down a few things I was looking for in a guy. Obviously, I want to date someone who shares my faith. But I realized there were other things that were important to me too.

My list changed over the years as I discovered new things about myself and put less emphasis on looks and more emphasis on the heart. But what I like about the list is that it keeps me from dating guys who are totally wrong for me! A guy doesn't have to fit every item on this list for me to date him, but if only a few match up, I know he's probably not the right one!

- Christian
- Spiritual leader
- Encourages others
- Weird humor (like me)
- Slow to anger
- Not super lazy
- Taller than me (or at least the same height)
- Understanding and forgiving heart
- Cleans up after himself
- Similar taste in music
- Attracted to him!
- Can cook (something other than mac 'n' cheese and popcorn)
- Expects me to be a working woman (even if that means I stay home with our kids for a few years first!)
- Genuine
- Has a good support system and guy friends in his life
- Doesn't want to change for me, but for Christ

is a source of life. It even says I can be an example to others as I live a pure life!

In my relationships, I have noticed that I can send the right message about my intentions for purity by dressing modestly and being honest about my boundaries. It's important to find relationships where you can respect each other's decisions and stick to them!

Stewardship. This is a fancy word that *Merriam-Webster* defines as "the careful and responsible management of something entrusted

Maybe you've heard the saying, "If you aim for nothing, you'll hit it every time!" Jotting down a simple list like this one can help you be wise about the kind of guy you date. Don't go crazy with fifty criteria he needs to meet, but list things that matter to you the most and can serve as a compass to your dating life.

to one's care." When you're in any kind of relationship with another person, whether it's a friendship, romantic relationship, or business partnership, you have a responsibility to love people well and try to do what's best for them.

When I'm in a relationship, I try to remember that if my boyfriend and I don't end up getting married, he will go on to have other relationships and likely marry someone else. Can I be proud of how I cared for him and built him up during our relationship? My goal is always that both of us would leave the relationship as better people than we were when it began.

HOW ROMANCE GOT BROKEN

Sometimes I like to think back to the garden of Eden, where God created the very first man and woman. The Bible doesn't tell us how long Adam was alone, but God saw that the poor guy was lonely, so he put him to sleep and took one of his ribs to create the woman. When Adam woke up, *voila!* A woman. Best. Present. Ever.

Think of how they must have enjoyed getting to know each other in that perfect place where there was no shame. Maybe they had dates where they walked over to the Eden Café for a couple of heavenly frappes. Or maybe they broke it down to some biblical hip-hop music. (Okay, maybe not.) They had been created for one another and were a true match made in heaven!

Then they disobeyed God, and everything changed. They had to leave the garden. They got sick, felt pain, and one day, they would die. Sin had made a mess of everything. And relationships were no exception.

Think about the relationships you've seen. I'm sure some of you have watched someone you know get divorced. Maybe you've been devastated by a bad breakup. Maybe you or someone you're close to got pregnant and is now a single mom. Relationships do not always work out in the way they should.

Dating has changed a lot in the last half century. Our grandparents went out on dates to the drive-in diner or movies with a different person every Saturday night until they found someone to "go steady" with. Today, couples "hang out," watching TV or movies, and sometimes casually fool around or hook up. There's a much greater emphasis on sex in dating relationships today, but we seem to have forgotten what God created sex for in the first place.

God designed sex for a husband and wife to become "one flesh" (Genesis 2:24). And according to science, when a couple has sex, they actually produce neurochemicals that make them feel bonded and even change their brains! This kind of connection is a huge benefit in marriage, because it gives you a special bond with your spouse. But introduce sex into a dating relationship, and things can get complicated *fast*.

We live in a culture that is obsessed with sex. As a society, we believe sex is our choice, our right, even our identity. Many people are comfortable having sex with no strings attached. A lot of people have also been hurt by the misuse of sex, through abuse and sexual assault. Something that God created to be special and beautiful has been trivialized or even corrupted in our world.

Because I grew up going to church, when I first started learning about sex, I heard a lot of reasons why I shouldn't do it before I was married. I could get a sexually transmitted infection; I could get pregnant; I could get my heart broken. And while all of those are great reasons to think twice about having sex, they aren't the most important reason to wait.

THE GREATEST RELATIONSHIP

When I was younger, I made an important decision: I decided that I would not have sex until I'm married. That may seem unusual to you, but let me tell you why I did it. God told me to. He didn't audibly speak to me, but as I read his Word, I learned that he didn't give me this rule to make me miss out on a special thing. He set boundaries for my protection and my good because he cares about me so deeply. Here are a few other things I learned about sex:

God wants the best for me. One of the biggest tensions with the "no sex" issue is feeling like I'm missing out on something good, especially when it seems like many people I know are making a different choice. I'm sure that sex is great. But God promises me that his ways are best. His plans for me are far better than my own. Psalm 18:30 says, "As for God, his way is perfect: The Lord's word is flawless." I can settle for what I think is good, or I can wait for God's best.

God designed sex for marriage. As far back as Adam and Eve, God created sex as a gift for married couples to enjoy, and a way for them to have children. As the creator of sex, God knows in what context it can be the very best. And that context is marriage.

Hebrews 13:4 says, "Marriage should be honored by all, and the marriage bed kept pure." One way I choose to keep my future marriage bed pure is to abstain from sex until I'm married.

Sexual purity honors God. This is true for both unmarried and married people. You would probably say it is wrong for a married person to cheat on her spouse by having sex with someone else, and you would be right! But using our sexuality in ways God says are right is important for all of us.

1 Corinthians 6:19–20 says: "Do you not know that your bodies are temples of the Holy Spirit, who is in you, whom you have received from God? You are not your own; you were bought at a price. Therefore honor God with your bodies." When I struggle with sexual temptation, I remember that Jesus has redeemed me. He loves me and I love him. And as I live for him in this area, I honor him.

I'm sure I'm not the only one who has made mistakes or pushed boundaries in this area of relationships. The good news is that God promises to make us new no matter what we have done (1 John 1:9). Every day I get to choose whether I will do things my own way or if I will do them God's way. And, for me, the main factor in that decision is my love for God and my desire to please him.

One of my friends used to struggle with compromising sexually in relationships. Even though she was a Christian, she says she was searching for her worth in the guys she dated. After one relationship where she did things she regretted, she felt God speaking to her. He said, "You can keep doing things your way, or you can do things my way." At that moment, she promised God she would do things his way because she knew that ultimately his plans for her were best.

As she followed God's guidelines for sex, she came to know and feel his love in a deeper way. She realized that he valued her more than a boyfriend ever could, and that he was always enough for her. Several years later, God provided her with a wonderful husband who had also chosen a pure lifestyle. Choosing to follow God faithfully in the years leading up to meeting her husband allowed my friend to enter marriage with joy.

A SINGLE SEASON

So I think that by now we can agree that romantic relationships are pretty amazing. It's no wonder that most of us long to have that special someone in our lives. But sometimes the timing is off.

Last year, a series of events led to a breakup with my boyfriend of seven months. We had been friends for a year before we dated. At first, it was really hard to not have him to lean on, talk to, and have fun with. But I noticed something: My relationship with God began to grow. A lot. When I found myself in a different situation, I was able to focus on a lot of things God was doing in my life.

When you are in a dating relationship, much of the growth you experience as a couple comes from each of you growing individually and then walking side by side. When you're single, you grow as an individual in preparation for that person God may bring to walk beside you. Singleness is never wasted, and it's definitely not a curse.

One day you may meet the person you want to spend your life with. And choices you make now will affect that relationship. So don't waste a moment! If you're in a relationship, learn and grow from it. And if you're single, practice the purity and wisdom you hope to bring to a relationship when it's the right time.

I've learned a lot since that very public sixth-grade kiss. God created us to live in relationship and give and receive love. There are a lot of ways relationships can go wrong, but there are also ways they can go very, very right. As we look to the one who gave us love in the first place, and seek to love others the way he does, romance and relationships can be one of the greatest things in life.

XOXO,

Chels

Insider Style Tip:

CREATING A GREAT DATE LOOK

"What should I wear?" is the big question when I'm going on a date. I try to decide what I'm going to wear the day before, so I'm not rushing right before my date. Here are a few guidelines for creating a killer date look:

Dress one step up. Dates are a great time to dress one step up from your normal attire. You don't have to be runway ready, but you can step outside your usual style. If you normally wear jeans and a hoodie, switch things up by wearing a skirt or a dress and boots. I also love to curl my hair or wear a sleek ponytail to step up my look for a date.

Accessorize. Going out calls for some awesome accents. Wear a scarf that makes your eyes pop, a hip jacket (a faux leather jacket looks amazing on everyone!), or jewelry that accents your outfit. Add cute color with a handbag or bright pair of shoes.

Mix up your makeup. If you're going on an evening date, don't be afraid to wear bold eye shadow or lip color (red is my favorite!). Focus on a makeup look that makes you feel pretty, while bringing out your best features. For a day date, play up your eyes and opt for a more natural lip.

The most important thing to remember when dressing for a date is to wear something that reflects your personality. You can't go wrong with being yourself!

CHAPTER 9

DOING THE HARD WORK

Be fearless in pursuit of what sets your soul on fire.

—UNKNOWN

When I was a kid, I wanted to be a dolphin trainer. Dolphins are my favorite animal, and I've always had a huge fascination with them. I loved watching trainers work with these gentle, intelligent creatures, and my ideal future included spending my days in the water doing the same.

I'm guessing that, like me, you've given some thought to your "dream job." Maybe when you were younger, you thought about being a ballerina on stage or an astronaut blasting off to the moon. Sometimes our earliest ideas of what we "want to be when we grow up" aren't exactly realistic. But they often do tap into something deep and real inside of us.

Even though a career in marine biology no longer seems likely, my love for these beautiful creatures is as strong as ever. Last year, while I was on vacation with my family in Florida, we rode jet skis one afternoon. When a few dolphins started swimming along with us, I started to cry. Crazy, right? They were just so beautiful, and this intense emotion washed over me!

What are you passionate about? Make a quick list in your head or jot down a few ideas here:

♥ _____

♥ _____

♥ _____

Having a passion for something—whether it's dolphins or make-up—is just the start of achieving your goals. Making your dreams a reality requires hard work and dedication as well. Accomplishing your goals (or even knowing what they should be) can seem really daunting.

QUOTES THAT MOTIVATE

When I'm feeling uninspired or weary, I love to read some great Christian authors to gain some motivation. Here are a few of my favorite quotes:

- "Faith does not eliminate questions. But faith knows where to take them."—Elisabeth Elliot
- "Radical obedience to Christ is not easy . . . It's not comfort, not health, not wealth, and not prosperity in this world. Radical obedience to Christ risks losing all these things. But in the end, such risk finds its reward in Christ. And he is more than enough for us."—David Platt
- "We fail in the work of grace and love when there is too much of us and not enough of God."—Suzanne Woods Fisher
- "Do not waste time bothering whether you 'love' your neighbor; act as if you did. As soon as we do this we find one of the great secrets. When you are behaving as if you loved someone you will presently come to love him."—C. S. Lewis
- "[I'm] a woman who wants to be more thankful for what I am than guilty for what I am not ... Cut the threads of guilt with grace."—Lysa TerKeurst

Sometimes young people get a bad reputation for not being able to commit to things or buckle down and do the hard work, and that can make even the most ambitious of us falter.

I know lots of people who grew up hearing that they could do anything they set their minds to. When you believe that's true—that all you have to do is have a dream—life can deliver some major disappointments. Dreams don't always work out. And you don't always see an immediate payoff for hard work.

I've learned that when you stick with something and don't give up, even when it's hard, you receive a sense of satisfaction for persisting with it, and hopefully you'll get some tangible rewards too. For example, last year I started running and ran regularly a few days each week. As I saw my body get stronger, I saw the payoff of my commitment and hard work.

Other times you may work hard at something and never experience any real success. I talked earlier about how my progress in gymnastics stalled when I was in middle school. At that time, I had to let my dreams of being a gymnast go and trust that God had a different plan for me. The work I put in up until that point didn't go to waste, however. I learned some great lessons about teamwork, self-discipline, and dedication.

The Bible actually talks a lot about work and how it leads to good things:

- "Be strong and do not give up, for your work will be rewarded." (2 Chronicles 15:7)
- "All hard work brings a profit, but mere talk leads only to poverty." (Proverbs 14:23)
- "The plans of the diligent lead to profit as surely as haste leads to poverty." (Proverbs 21:5)

You can't just talk about doing something; you actually have to do it! Even though there will be times when you're not excited to do your homework or head to your job or hit the gym, God actually created you to work. That's right. He gave Adam, the first human, jobs to do in the garden. And when Adam and Eve left the garden, work became essential to their survival. We aren't meant to sit around and binge on Netflix or stay in bed all day. In fact, working is what makes our moments of rest or fun all the more enjoyable. And if you are someone who has a dream, or a goal, or even just the beginning of an idea, get used to the concept of working hard to make your dreams a reality.

HOW I LEARNED TO WORK IT

Getting a million and a half subscribers to my YouTube channel is not something that happened overnight. There was a lot of planning and work involved. When I first started my channel, I didn't have goals or even much drive. (I was a typical eighth grader!) I posted videos because it was fun and I was interested in makeup. The process was simple back then too: I recorded a video on my computer, put some music behind it in iMovie, and uploaded it to my channel. Boom. Done!

But as my channel's popularity began to grow, so did the expectation for better quality and more quantity of online content. I'm really thankful that my mom and dad supported me (and pushed me a little) during that transition, because, at times, the amount of work involved was daunting. I had to get organized in order to meet all of the demands that came with being a YouTuber.

Here is how my system for producing regular content works today. I think you can apply parts of the process to whatever goals you may be pursuing.

Brainstorming: Each month, I create a list of videos I hope to post. I put the ideas in an order based on seasonal considerations or current trends. Planning and setting goals are important parts of succeeding at any activity.

Filming: My dad and I spend an hour to two hours filming each video. Sometimes it requires setting up three different cameras or going out to a particular location to shoot. Every time we film, my

dad also takes regular photos to use as thumbnails and to post on all of my social media outlets. (I have to make sure that I'm posting original content on each platform for those who follow me on all of them.) Maybe you're learning to be proficient at an instrument or training for a sport. This step of the process is about doing the actual work and putting in the practice.

Editing: I spend three to eight hours editing each video. During this process, I pare down the footage, and add music, transitions, and effects. I still do all of my own editing, because the way that you edit something infuses a lot of your personality into it. Editing is the part of the process that has helped me get really good at what I do. Once you're putting in the time to achieve your goals, you have to hone your skills. Sometimes this means looking for new opportunities and taking some risks.

Uploading: When a video is ready to go, I schedule it to upload to my YouTube channel. I post up to three new videos a week! If you want to get good at something, you have to be consistent. Whether you work out five days a week, schedule an hour a day for piano practice, hit the books every night after dinner, or even commit to a daily Bible reading plan, consistency brings results.

Posting: On top of creating and uploading videos, I have to produce regular content for Instagram, Twitter, Facebook, and Snapchat. I try to post original content—which includes photos, inspirational quotes, and beauty or life advice—on each of those outlets. That way, people who follow me on multiple platforms get fresh content on each one. In order to have advice to share, I do a lot of reading and research behind the scenes.

You may not be posting on social media the way I do, but you have to find a way to share your life and passions with others. Maybe this means being part of a team or a club with people pursuing similar goals. You may join a play to further your acting ambitions. Or if you're a writer, maybe you work for the school yearbook or newspaper to experience working with a staff of writers. You can't accomplish your goals in a vacuum (more on that soon!).

As you can see, keeping my channel going requires a lot of organization and effort! If I'm going on vacation, I have to work extra hard to complete videos before I leave, so I can enjoy my time with family or friends. There are weeks when I have worked thirty-five hours in four days!

This is a great place to point out that I *cannot* accomplish my goals alone. I need help! Long ago, I figured out that I can't physically do all of the work my channel requires. So I brought in trusted people to help me. I've already mentioned my dad, who is my rock star film and photography crew all in one. But I've also hired some of my friends who are great at writing and editing to help provide content for my website.

Three of my close friends write short articles each week that we post as daily content on the website. These ladies are up to date on fashion trends and beauty info, but they also know me and the types of things I like to post. Not only do they work for me, but these women are also amazing encouragers. When my website hit a million views, we went out to a fancy restaurant in St. Louis to celebrate. I could not keep all of my platforms going without this team!

Even with help, keeping up with all of my responsibilities has been difficult, especially when I'm in school. There have been a few times when I've stayed up all night editing a video and still had to get up and go to class the next day.

Remember how I said I didn't have a lot of drive when I first started my channel? Well, as BeautyLiciousInsider grew, and especially as I began sharing more videos about the things I was passionate about, my desire to put in the effort also grew. Those all-nighters flew by because I was so excited about getting a video uploaded the next day!

WHEN YOU DON'T SEE THE PAYOFF

A few years after I started my channel, my diligence really started to pay off. I collaborated on some videos with my brother, Chandler, and some of those videos received more than a million views! Offers to represent brands, appear in magazines, and even star in TV shows were pouring in faster than I could respond. The number of views on each video sky-rocketed! I felt like my newfound super-success would last forever.

Around that time, I started to post some videos about topics I was

THE WORLD'S DREAMS VS. GOD'S DREAMS

Having dreams and goals is kind of a big deal in our culture. You've probably heard an athlete or celebrity talk about how a certain accomplishment or award is the fulfillment of a dream. But the world's ideas about what we should strive for, and the things that will make as happy, are sometimes very different than God's ideas. And his plans for us are always better. Here are a few comparisons:

THE WORLD SAYS . . .	GOD SAYS . . .
You only live once, so do everything you can to find fulfillment in this life and the things of this world.	You can live forever, and the things of this world are not worth comparing to the great joy of the life to come that I offer.
Do whatever makes you happy. Live for the moment.	My thoughts are higher than your thoughts and my ways are higher than your ways (Isaiah 55:9). Sometimes, in the moment, my ways won't seem like they bring "happiness," but they will fill your heart with peace and joy.
"Fame is the aim" and you should always get the credit for the things you do.	Your primary goal is to be a servant to everyone; your rewards will be in heaven.
Wealth and material things will make you happy and give you security.	Wealth and material things do not last. Pursuing me and my plans for you will always give you joy and security.

really passionate about, such as living for Christ, overcoming temptation, and studying the Bible. Even though I was hearing that the faith videos were really helping some people, the posts received far fewer views than the ones about makeup or fashion.

It was discouraging to see the number of views dip on some of my videos. It kind of felt like being in a popularity contest—and I was losing. I had a decision to make: I could craft all of my content to bring in the most views I possibly could (I knew the types of videos my subscribers went nuts over), or I could post content that was true to myself and refuse to let the number of views or comments define me.

I decided to stick to my gut. I continued to post those faith videos in order to reflect myself and what I want to tell the world. It hasn't always been easy. Even when you're doing what you know is right, some of your choices won't be popular. But I've discovered that God rewards us for being faithful to what he is asking us to do, even if the result doesn't look like "success" to those around us.

As I've chosen to stay faithful in posting the type of content I feel called to post, I've seen a lot of different opportunities come my way that may not have happened otherwise. I've been invited to speak at churches, I appeared in a faith-based movie, and I even had the chance to write this book! Choosing to not focus on numbers gave me the freedom to be creative and explore new avenues where God might use me. Plus, as I've continued to post advice, the number of subscribers interested in that content has increased.

CHASING YOUR DREAMS

In the early days of my channel, I wasn't super passionate about what I was doing. I think that's because I didn't find true fulfillment in it. Sure, it was fun making videos and telling other girls how to style their hair or do their makeup, but I knew I wasn't doing something that would last and keep me satisfied. I was pretty much aiming for the "American Dream" of being successful and doing whatever made me happy.

But when I posted my Christian testimony video, my thinking began to change. I heard from many people who said my story had really made a difference in their lives. The more I posted those kinds of videos, the more certain I became that *this* is what God had intended for my YouTube channel all along.

As I've gotten to know God better, he has replaced some of my smaller dreams with the greater dream of being part of the work he is doing in the world. That gives me more purpose than I know what to do with sometimes! And it motivates me to work hard, because I'm doing something that matters.

That may sound a little strange to you, and it kind of is. God's ways are very different from our own. Sometimes he calls us to do things that don't seem to make sense or even line up with our original passions.

If you had asked me a few years ago for advice on achieving your dreams, I would have said, "Just go for it! Go after whatever you feel passionate about! You can do it." Those words are still partially true. But during the past few years, God has radically changed my views on this topic. For me, pursuing my dreams and pursuing Christ are inseparable. Listen to what Psalm 37:4 has to say: "Take delight in the Lord, and he will give you the desires of your heart." The more deeply I fall in love with Jesus, the more he makes me feel satisfied in the things I am doing.

I've learned that God doesn't take away your dreams. It's more like he reshapes them to be even better than the dreams you had in the first place. I once dreamed of getting a certain number of views on my videos, or reaching a certain level of popularity on YouTube, but God's plan involved me playing a role in how he reached and changed people's hearts! God's plan was so much bigger than my own.

I have a friend named Nick, who likes fast cars as much as I do. He was actually planning to pursue a career in racing, but he felt God calling him into full-time ministry instead. Nick describes the experience as a "tug-of-war" when it came to letting go of his own dreams. Eventually, Nick realized that God had a bigger plan for him, so he changed direction.

I'm not saying that God's plan for everyone is going to be full-time ministry. Lots of people are a light for Christ in the regular workforce. God could have easily chosen Nick to be a light to other race car drivers! The point is that God may have something different for you than you envisioned for yourself.

So what do you do if you don't know what your passions are or have no idea what you should be doing with your life? Don't be discouraged! I've been there. As a senior in high school, I really had no idea what I should do next. I decided to enroll in college like a lot of my friends were doing. I didn't know what to study, exactly, so I chose the field of communications, hoping that over time I'd pick a major. I still didn't really know what I wanted to be when I grew up.

Although I planned my course, God drastically redirected my steps. Two weeks into school, I started dealing with depression and anxiety (more about that in the next chapter). Although I tried to figure out a way to stay in school, it soon became apparent that I needed to move home. Even though I knew that God was directing my steps, it was still a scary time filled with unknowns.

Maybe you've been through something like that—an unwanted detour or a major stall on your dreams. In those moments, where you feel like you don't have any control, there are two important things you can do.

Draw close to God. One of the best ways to uncover passions is to pursue a relationship with God. As you get to know him better, you will discover new things about yourself and who he has created you to be. As I have grown in my relationship with Christ, he has given me a stronger desire to encourage others who may be struggling with some of the same problems and temptations I've dealt with. That desire has guided my work, how I spend my time, and even what I hope to do in the future.

Be faithful where you are. Many of us live pretty ordinary lives when you think about it. We go to school, work, watch TV, eat, hang out with family and friends, and repeat. My life may look glamorous on YouTube, but as I've already mentioned, you're more likely to find me behind a computer screen than out on the town. A verse that has encouraged me to be faithful in my everyday living is 1 Corinthians 10:31, where Paul writes, "So whether you eat or drink or whatever you do, do it all for the glory of God." You don't have to have big, fancy dreams to make a difference! Even mundane activities can be done in ways that bring glory to God.

My life has changed a lot since I dreamed of becoming a dolphin trainer. I still have many of the same passions I had then, but some of my deepest desires have been revealed as I pursue Christ. I've done things I never would have thought possible back then. And while it has been a ton of fun, it has also taken a lot of hard work.

Over time, I've come to appreciate work because I see how it accomplishes amazing things in my life and in the lives of others. As I set my eyes on Christ and do my best to be faithful in the small things, he allows me to do more than I ever dreamed possible. So go ahead and chase your dreams. You can do more than you think you can. But always chase him first.

XOXO,

Chels

Insider Beauty Tip:

MASTERING DIFFICULT TECHNIQUES

Some makeup and hair techniques are easier to do than others. For example, applying mascara is somewhat simple to master, while applying false eyelashes can take some practice. I'm pretty much a "no hassle" type of girl, so I'm rather selective when it comes to the complicated techniques I spend time on. But here are a few that I think are worth the extra effort:

Contouring. It took me a long time to figure out how to contour my round face, using bronzer to give my face definition. Once I mastered the technique, though, I loved how it made my face appear slimmer. I typically take a matte bronzer and apply it slightly above my cheekbones *before* I apply my normal foundation. This gives structure but also doesn't appear too bold once I apply the foundation.

Dressing well. I used to be pretty bad at putting together a look. I lacked confidence when it came to combining articles of clothing to create an outfit. (I look back at old photos and cringe at what I used to pair

together!) What helped was using Instagram as a source of inspiration and following influencers who dressed in cute, fun ways. I also began paying close attention to colors and how they complimented each other. Fashion is definitely an art, because you're pairing colors and textures together to create a unique look! Your style will evolve over time—but no matter where you are on your fashion journey, learning the color wheel can take your looks to a whole new level.

Curling my hair. I love the way my hair looks when it's curled! But learning to curl my mane was frustrating at first, because I have so much hair. I use a wand to get the job done faster, but some days it still seems to take forever. But becoming skilled at curling has definitely helped make the process less of a chore. I try to give myself plenty of time when I curl my hair so I don't feel rushed. I start by focusing on the front pieces so I get the instant gratification of seeing the look start to come together. As I get toward the back of my head, I curl bigger sections of hair. Sometimes curls fall out and turn into waves, which I personally like.

CHAPTER 10

WHEN LIFE GETS YOU DOWN

Difficult roads often lead to beautiful destinations.

—UNKNOWN

The summer after my senior year of high school was one of the best of my life. It began with a fun-filled vacation to Florida with my family, and only got better from there. The balmy summer nights were filled with laughter and talking as I spent time with friends before we headed off to college. Life was filled with anticipation as I thought ahead to the upcoming adventure of going to a Christian college in sunny California; I would be near the beach and surrounded by new friends who shared my faith and love for life.

At the end of the summer, I squeezed as much of my stuff as I possibly could into my little red Camaro and set out on an epic 1,800-mile road trip with my dad. The drive was amazing. My dad and I had so many great conversations, the scenery was magnificent, and we stopped at some incredible spots along the way. An online post from August 31, 2016, captures the excitement I felt:

"There have been so many moments this week that God has shown himself in immense ways. I truly believe he blessed this trip, and I am so excited to move in tomorrow! From stunning heat lightning the first night we drove, to sitting on the edge of a rock looking down into the Grand Canyon, it's been so fun. Thank you to those who have been praying for this new adventure of mine and those who simply follow my life. I am so, *so* thankful for each one of you."

When I got to college and moved into the dorm, everything was even better than I expected. During move-in weekend, the school threw this giant party to help students get to know each other. At one point I was dancing and rapping along to one of my favorite Lecrae songs, and a bunch of people formed a circle around me. It was amazing. For the first time ever, I felt like I truly belonged. I had found my people!

That first week of school was packed with fun experiences—decorating my dorm room, making new friends, visiting a new church. I even did a dorm room tour video for my channel. I felt on top of the world, like I could do or be anything.

THE CRASH

I don't exactly know how to describe what happened next, but it was like I was skiing and hit a tree. Toward the beginning of my second week at college, I woke up one morning and felt unmotivated to do anything. I just wanted to stay in bed. I couldn't look at my homework without panicking. I had no appetite. And anything I did eat came right back up.

I sensed something was really wrong, but I knew college freshmen commonly felt overwhelmed and homesick during the first few weeks of college, so I tried to ignore what I was feeling and just push through. The problem with that was, everything felt exponentially harder to do than it had before. I couldn't figure out how to tackle even the simplest of problems. Anxiety constantly washed over me. It felt like I was sliding downhill, and I couldn't figure out how to scramble back up. I found out later that I was experiencing the classic symptoms of clinical depression.

I never thought I would be a person who struggled with depression. I've always been the type of girl who is upbeat no matter what. And yet, there I was. One day I was super happy, having fun with new people and feeling like my life was the greatest, and the next day I felt like I'd been hit by a train. Somehow there was a big old chink in my armor, and all these demoralizing thoughts began running through my head. *You're going to fail college. You'll never make any true friends.* I was in such a low place, physically and emotionally, that I believed the lies.

TRUTH FOR HARD TIMES

When I'm going through a hard time, I often seek comfort in Scripture. Here are a few of my favorite verses for going through trials. Try writing one of these verses on a card and hanging it in a place you look often.

- "God is our refuge and strength, an ever-present help in trouble."—Psalm 46:1
- "In all this you greatly rejoice, though now for a little while you may have had to suffer grief in all kinds of trials."—1 Peter 1:6
- "When you pass through the waters, I will be with you; and when you pass through the rivers, they will not sweep over you. When you walk through the fire, you will not be burned; the flames will not set you ablaze."—Isaiah 43:2
- "In all your ways submit to him, and he will make your paths straight."—Proverbs 3:6
- "Put your hope in the Lord."—Psalm 130:7

On Friday morning, I woke up with a chilling thought: I just want all of this pain to go away. I don't want to live like this anymore.

Recognizing the danger in my thinking, I immediately called my dad and mom and told them I needed to come home. We decided I would fly home for the weekend and decide what to do from there.

When I went home, I thought that my problems would all go away. But they didn't. I still could barely eat, and I would start to cry for no reason. On top of the physical struggles, I felt heartbroken because my college plans hadn't worked out. All of my friends were off having a great time at school, and I was the one who had to come home. I felt ashamed and confused about what to do next.

THE TRUTH ABOUT TRIALS

We live in a broken world. Every person experiences trials and suffering of some kind in this life. Maybe someone you loved died or you struggle with a serious health issue. Maybe your mom and dad got a divorce or your boyfriend dumped you. You may have trouble making friends or get bullied at school.

Our trials may look different, but they all cause pain. Here are a few different types of hard times you may experience in your life:

Troubles. Have you ever felt as if things just aren't going your way? Your car breaks down. You fail a test. You get sick and miss a special event. All of these troubles are minor in and of themselves, but they can still ruin your day or week.

Hardship. Maybe you've been going through a series of troubles for an extended period of time. Your dad lost his job. Someone you love is sick. Your family struggles to pay the bills and make ends meet. Sometimes it can seem as if one thing after another goes wrong and relief is never going to come.

Pain. Whether you suffer from a physical ailment or the emotional fallout from trauma or a broken relationship, pain can be difficult to deal with. Going through life with pain of any kind is draining, and can make it difficult to cope with any challenge that's happening at the same time.

Persecution. People can face persecution for many different reasons, including who they are and what they believe. Mistreatment by others can also come as a result of following Jesus or doing what is right. It may be something obvious, like being teased or bullied for taking an unpopular stand, or it may be less direct, such as being excluded from certain groups or opportunities because of your beliefs.

Whether your trials are major or minor, they have the potential to steal your joy and sidetrack you from God's plans. We shouldn't be surprised when we go through hard things. Jesus told his followers, "In this world you will have trouble. But take heart! I have overcome the world" (John 16:33). I know that may not seem especially helpful when you're going through the pains and struggles of your daily life, but it is the reason we can have hope in any circumstance, even the really difficult ones.

When I was at my lowest point with depression, I was reminded that God was still at work and had a bigger plan and purpose than I could see. That knowledge helped me get through the hard days. As strange as it sounds, trials can actually come with some pretty big benefits. Here are a few that come to mind:

Trials can draw us closer to God. I have talked to many people who either met God during a hard time or learned to depend on him more through a major challenge. When I first had to leave college, I felt distant from God and asked him why these things were happening to me. But as I chose to trust him, even when I couldn't understand the "why" behind it all, he began revealing himself to me in new ways and gave me a thirst to know him more deeply. I ended up feeling closer to him in my hard times than I had during all the happy moments I'd experienced the previous summer.

Trials produce maturity. There are some interesting words about trials in the book of James: "Consider it pure joy, my brothers and sisters, whenever you face trials of many kinds" (verse 2). Um, wait a minute. Does that sound a little crazy to you? I don't think I've ever welcomed a trial with *pure joy*! But James continues: "[T]he testing of your faith produces perseverance. Let perseverance finish its work so that you may be mature and complete, not lacking anything" (verse 3). Sometimes the only way you will grow in the ways God desires is through a trial. My hardest times have developed patience and strength in me that I didn't even know existed! And many times, when a trial is over, I have a very different perspective on life than before it began.

Trials help us to help others. Have you ever been going through something hard and someone seems to say the perfect thing at the perfect time? You may find out that he or she's been through the

FOUR WAYS TO OVERCOME BUMPS IN THE ROAD

Sometimes life can really get you down. Here are four ways to rise above trials:

1. **Do something positive.** When I was feeling low, I started running. The regular workouts gave me a chance to clear my head and also focus on what I love about life—fresh air, the beauty of God's creation, and a healthy body that can run! Running also helped with some of the physical things going on with my body that were contributing to my depression.

2. **Focus on the big picture.** Just because you're going through something hard now, it doesn't mean that you couldn't be in a totally different (and better) place even a few months down the road! God uses trials to mold us, and when we keep our eye on the prize—the full life God promises his children and our glorious future with him—some of the everyday hardships fade in comparison. Try making a list of things happening in the next several months that you're looking forward to.

same—or a similar—experience. The Bible talks about this. God is compassionate and generous with comfort when his children go through hard times! He even consoles us when our pain is the result of our own poor choices. There's a reason for this: He comforts us in our troubles so that we can likewise comfort others well and show his love and compassion for us to our neighbor (2 Corinthians 1:4).

Before I experienced depression myself, I didn't feel like I could easily talk to someone who was going through it. But now God is opening doors for me to comfort others who battle depression and anxiety. Knowing that God could use my pain to help someone else gave me a lot of solace when my days seemed dark.

Trials don't last forever. This one is especially good news to me. Even the worst pain fades over time. Sometimes, it goes away completely. You may not be able to see a light at the end of the tunnel

3. **Spend time with good people.** If you're feeling down, your first instinct may be to withdraw from people. But good friends, who will encourage you, are the best people to surround yourself with when life gets hard. Family can also be a great support. They can give you perspective, offer a shoulder to cry on, and help you see the silver lining.

4. **Don't be afraid to get help.** If you can't seem to shake your doldrums, or you develop other symptoms of depression—such as a loss of appetite, sleep disruption, or a lack of interest in things you used to enjoy doing—go to your doctor. One of the healthiest things I did when I was experiencing depression was to go to a doctor right away. I also started seeing a counselor who could give me practical tools for dealing with my depression. Even if your troubles are less serious, don't hesitate to seek out a mentor or pastor to talk with.

today, or tomorrow, or next week, but it's there. 1 Peter 5:10 says, "And the God of all grace, who called you to his eternal glory in Christ, after you have suffered a little while, will himself restore you and make you strong, firm and steadfast." What an amazing promise!

Bad things will happen in this life and hard times will come. But through it all, God is with us, using each trial that comes our way for our good and his glory.

I like how Frank Peretti, the *New York Times* bestselling author of *No More Bullies*, says in that book, "God does not waste an ounce of our pain or a drop of our tears; suffering doesn't come our way for no reason, and he seems especially efficient at using what we endure to mold our character. If we are malleable, he takes our bumps and bruises and shapes them into something beautiful."

Trials can produce positive things—such as love, joy, and incredible peace in our lives—because God can redeem anything. Whether a hardship is the result of our own choices or something completely outside of our control, God will walk through it with us and bring beauty out of the ashes. That is big comfort during hard times.

AN UNWANTED DETOUR

When I went home from college, I assumed my depression would clear up and things would go back to normal. I was looking for a quick fix. Especially because when I had faced a problem in the past, my go-to approach was to figure it out and take care of it right away. I just wasn't able to do that this time. Instead, things got worse before they got better.

I broke up with my boyfriend around the same time. My dad lost his job. And I was still grieving the loss of my college dreams. Many days I felt hopeless and could barely sleep or eat. I went to see a counselor, which was one of the best decisions I made. She helped me examine the root issues contributing to my anxiety and depression, and gave me tools to work through both.

Even though I wanted to trust God during that time, I found it very hard to connect with him at first. He seemed so distant, and I didn't understand why these things were happening to me. But I just kept trying to seek him. I continued reading my Bible and praying and trusting that God had a purpose in what I was going through.

After a few weeks, I began to see glimpses of hope. Some days I felt like myself again. I even saw some good starting to come from my move

back to Illinois. My family began attending church together, something we hadn't done for years. And this resulted in some great conversations with new friends from church.

As I started to feel better, I discovered contentment in the Lord and the path he had chosen for me. I could tell I was growing in my relationship with him more than I had before all of these "bad things" happened. I sensed God was doing things in me that he could only do through the trials I was experiencing.

He began putting people in my life who shared my faith and values and could encourage me. I felt renewed passion and joy in the work I was doing on YouTube and this book—even though I was 1,800 miles away from where I'd expected to be. God was rewriting my story, but I could see that he had a bigger purpose in it, and whatever happened would be beautiful. I witnessed many amazing things that could only be explained by God being at work.

BEAUTIFULLY BROKEN

Struggling with depression and leaving college isn't the only hard thing I've gone through. When I was ten years old, my parents experienced a difficult time in their marriage. They had some serious issues they needed to work through, and there was almost constant tension and fighting in our home. I was terrified that my parents would get a divorce. I remember taking my younger siblings into another room when my parents argued and turning up music really loud to block out the noise.

That experience was a lot for my ten-year-old brain and heart to process. I am so thankful that my parents were able to work things out and forgive each other. God intervened in some big ways, bring-ing Christian friends alongside my parents to encourage them to stay together.

They didn't get a divorce, and our family came out stronger on the other side. I even learned some valuable lessons about commitment and forgiveness. But the helplessness, fear, and anger I felt during that trial didn't go away for a long time. For years after, it affected my view of marriage and even my relationship with my parents.

All of us go through things that "break" us. The break may be a small chip or a crack, or it may be more like shattering into a million pieces and then having to be glued back together. Some wounds are so deep that only Christ can bring the healing and forgiveness we need to move on. But when we invite him into our pain, he not only has the ability to heal us, he can also use us in extraordinary ways.

I recently heard someone say that when we walk through trials in an honest, transparent way, we are kind of like a cracked coffee mug. The cracks, though repaired, allow the light of Christ to shine out of us. Remember the childhood song that goes, "This little light of mine, I'm gonna let it shine"? Well, hard times in our lives can illuminate Jesus in ways our happier times can't. People may wonder why we have hope when we're broken, and that wonder could lead them to discover something new in their own lives.

LIGHT IN THE DARKNESS

When I was in sixth grade, my family and I were on our way to church one day when we saw a big commotion up ahead. The church parking lot was filled with emergency vehicles, and police officers were turning vehicles around. Later that day we found out that our pastor had been shot while he was preaching the sermon at the first service. A man who was mentally ill had walked into the church (where 150 people were worshiping), approached the pastor, and began shooting.

Pastor Fred held up his Bible for protection, and those who were there said the shots going through the Bible looked like confetti. Some people even wondered if it was an elaborate act as part of the sermon. It wasn't; Pastor Fred was killed. Our church was devastated. It just seemed unreal that something so horrible happened at our small church . . . to our pastor!

I will never forget how Fred's wife handled the tragedy, though.

Even though she was left a widow with two young daughters, she forgave the man who killed her husband. And even as she healed from her heartbreak, her deep trust in God and unshakeable faith brought many people closer to him.

When I go through hard times, I want to be like Pastor Fred's wife. I want people to wonder at the hope that I have. Light shines the brightest into darkness, after all.

God can bring beautiful things out of the most hopeless circumstances. And he promises a day is coming when there will be no more tears or pain. So if you're in a dark place today, remember that light is already shining in. Keep going. Keep holding on. God's got this.

XOXO,

Chels

Insider Style Tip:

EASY LOOKS FOR COLLEGE

I may not be in the college scene at the moment, but I'm always on the hunt for quick, versatile looks my friends can use at school. Here are a few of my favorites:

THE "I JUST WOKE UP, BUT YOU CAN'T TELL" LOOK

Outfit: Black leggings, oversized sweater, ankle booties, and ruffle socks.

Hair: Gather all your hair together like you're putting it into a high ponytail, then start twisting the hair into a bun. Secure the casual "messy bun" with elastics and bobby pins.

Makeup: Sometimes I'm in such a rush that I skip makeup completely. But to achieve a look that's a bit more "together," dust a powder foundation over your face, add some mascara, and apply a lip plumper. *Bam!* Done!

THE "I JUST GOT ASKED OUT BY A GUY IN MY BIOLOGY CLASS" LOOK

Outfit: Black jeans, beige blouse, dainty choker necklace, and fun wedges.

Hair: Braid your hair in small braids the night before, then take them out when you wake up to reveal wavy, crimped hair!

Makeup: Full face of makeup including rosy blush, a natural eye, and a pop of maroon or earth tones on the lips.

THE "I LOOK LIKE I WORK OUT EVERY DAY" LOOK

Outfit: Purple athletic-style pullover, black sweatpants, and gray running shoes.

Hair: Brush through your hair, and either leave it down and natural, put it into a ponytail, or braid it into two sections.

Makeup: Minimal makeup including mascara, a nude shadow to conceal redness or discoloration around eyes, and a berry lip balm.

CHAPTER 11

THE REAL ME

A flower does not think of competing with the flower next to it. It just blooms.

—UNKNOWN

Sometimes I forget that I haven't exactly lived a normal life. Posting that first video to YouTube when I was thirteen changed the course of my life in ways I never could have anticipated. After all, my original motivation was the passion I had for makeup and having fun online.

I know a lot of people dream about being a celebrity or even simply being popular at school. In many ways, I've experienced those things. After I placed second at the NYX Face Awards, my follower count soared and a lot of opportunities opened up. I still felt like a pretty average teen, but a few not-normal perks of the job began coming my way. For example, I started receiving free makeup and beauty products in the mail almost every week!

Having so many people interested in me and my channel has been overwhelming at times. The attention can be nice, but in those early days

I had to make big decisions about who I was going to be and what I was going to build my life around.

IDENTITY CRISIS

Even though I do feel rather ordinary most of the time, there's no doubt that my YouTube career has provided me with some really cool experiences and extra attention. Having thousands of people like and comment on everything you put online can be pretty weird and cool at the same time.

When my channel first became popular, I struggled with finding my worth and identity in the popularity of my posts and even feeling prideful about my success. All of the attention was exhilarating, but after a while, I realized that getting views and likes online wasn't fulfilling; I always wanted more. I knew if I kept trying to feed myself with the recognition and approval of other people, I would never be satisfied.

STAR TREATMENT

My day-to-day life is pretty normal, but there are a few "perks" to being an online celebrity.

Free makeup. Almost every week, I get shipments of makeup from companies like Smashbox, Tarte, and Neutrogena. I always have a supply of the latest cosmetics, which is pretty cool. There is no way I can use it all, however, so sometimes I give it away as gifts. Other times I find something I really enjoy using.

Special events. In my line of work, I get invited to a lot of special events, such as conventions, festivals, and conferences. A few years ago, I represented Mattel at BeautyCon in New York. I received this opportunity after I made a Barbie makeup tutorial that received an incredible 17 million views.

Commercials. I have a long-standing partnership with Neutrogena. I love their eye-makeup remover and skincare products. A few years ago, I did a commercial for Neutrogena with actress Bella Thorne that was featured all over YouTube. It was a cool experience to be on set and see how a commercial was made. Sometimes I make mini commercials for my social media in order to feature different products.

Free food. Here's some insider information: People get paid to scour social media for certain brand or product names. Every time you tweet or hashtag something on social media, you can be confident that companies will discover what you're saying about them! One time I tweeted, "I love jalapeño Kettle Chips!" The next thing I knew, the company that makes the chips saw my tweet and sent me a DM, telling me they would love to send me some of their chips. A few days later, I received boxes full of Kettle Chips in every flavor!

Red carpet treatment. When I was seventeen, Alexandra and John Graham—a couple who writes, directs, and produces faith-based films—approached me about auditioning for their holiday movie *Wish for Christmas*. I had never been in a movie before, or even done much acting aside from my own videos on YouTube. I ended up getting a role as a friend of the lead character, and when the movie was released, I went to Los Angeles for the premiere. It was awesome!

I still struggle with this sometimes. I've caught myself checking Twitter just to see how many retweets I've received on a certain post. Sure, doing so helps me to see what resonates with my followers, but it can quickly turn into a nasty habit of tweeting things just for the recognition. What can follow is believing that the success is all because of me. But since I gave my life to Christ, I know that my success and all the amazing opportunities I've had come from him.

When I do find myself caring too much about likes and views, I shift my focus to what is real. I remind myself that my true value has nothing to do with my online success. I am significant based on the fact God created me and calls me his beloved child! I have family and friends who'd love for me to unplug and spend quality time with them. And I still have tons of new experiences to explore outside the world of retweets and shares.

Maybe you have experienced success in a certain area. Perhaps you're great at a sport or really smart in school. Or you may be popular at school or have a great job. As much as it feels good to excel at something—and the people around you may make a big deal about it— your true value has nothing to do with your accomplishments. Instead, your value has *everything* to do with who you are.

I had to realize that even if I was reaching only one person (or none!), I would still be as valuable to God as I am with this huge online following. That can be hard to wrap my head around sometimes. When I start to get down because I'm losing subscribers or people don't like what I'm doing, I ask the question, "Is this going to matter next year or even next month?" If the answer is no, it's not worth fretting over.

Whenever I start questioning my value, I like to write down a few things that are part of who I am, not what I've done or how I look. I encourage you to write down three to five things that are part of your personal identity right now! Go ahead—scribble them down in this book if you need to. I don't mind!

Here are some examples of things I've written down about myself in the past:

- I am funny.
- I am smart.
- I am good at communicating.
- I have a great family.
- I am a Christian.

Now, next to each thing you wrote about yourself, write "might change" or "won't change." Here's an example: I have realized that my popularity on YouTube probably won't last forever—it might change—but my relationship with Christ will last forever—it won't change. As we go through life, it's important to focus on the parts of our identity that won't change. These are the things worth investing our time and effort into.

Have you ever lost a piece of your identity? Maybe it was a relationship, or a skill, or an opportunity you were expecting to have. Giving up something that makes you "you" can be devastating and even create an identity crisis. At moments like those, you are forced to ask yourself the question, "Who am I now?"

When I had to drop out of college after only two weeks, I was faced with this question. Throughout my senior year of high school, I had planned and dreamed about going off to college. I have always been a person who loves to relate to people through shared experiences, and since a lot of teens go to college directly after high school, doing the same seemed like a perfect way to connect with my subscribers and show them the importance of education. Plus, let's be honest: I wanted to prove to people that I could do it.

Obviously, God had different plans, but the loss of something I

TEN SURPRISING THINGS ABOUT ME

1. I *love* cars, specifically sports cars. I have a 2015 Camaro that's my baby.
2. I'm actually decent at ice skating (and roller skating). I used to play hockey when I was little, so my skills have carried on into adulthood.
3. I'm looking forward to having my own boys someday. For some reason, I love babysitting little boys; they're so energetic, but also easy to handle.
4. I'm actually an introvert. I may be on my A game when I meet subscribers and get in front of the camera, but I love my quiet time every day and recharge when I'm by myself.
5. I have three dogs. Two of them are Shar-Peis (the cutest, wrinkliest dogs in the world), and we also have an adorable black lab.
6. I used to have super curly hair, but as I've gotten older it's gone stick straight.
7. I hardly ever paint my nails. I seriously have *so much* nail polish, but I prefer to wear my nails natural.
8. My mom yells at me nearly every day for wearing mismatched socks, but I don't believe in matching pairs.
9. I used to beat all the boys in basketball in middle school, and I'm still proud of that.
10. I used to be insecure about the shape of my face, but now I love it.

envisioned myself doing forced me to reevaluate who I was apart from that. I wasn't going to be "Chelsea, successful YouTube personality, who conquers college in a single bound." I was going to be something—or someone—else. Someone new. And at the beginning, that person was yet to be determined.

PRESSURE TO PERFORM

So what shapes our identity, our sense of who we are? The two biggest outward influences are the people in our lives and our accomplishments.

Studies reveal that young people today are more stressed out and anxious than any previous generation. Much of that stress comes from the pressure to do well in school so you can get into a good college so you can ultimately get a good job. (And, as our culture likes to tell us, to be rich and successful.) Juggling school, extracurriculars, friends, and more can be seriously stressful. And that's just at school!

I've felt this kind of pressure myself as I've struggled to balance my YouTube career with school, family life, and friendships. I'm not usually too hard on myself, but when I really care about something, I can be a perfectionist and put a ton of effort into getting it just right.

I also sometimes feel pressure from people around me to work harder, do more, or produce better content. The world we live in puts a lot of emphasis on achievement and success, and we can feel like we always have to do more and more to be accepted by people or even by God. But God cares about who I am, not what I can do.

One of my favorite stories from the Bible is about two sisters named Mary and Martha, who were friends with Jesus when he lived on earth. Pretty cool, right? One day Jesus came over to their house for dinner. Now, Martha was the type who wanted to be the perfect hostess. From her perspective, there were a million things she needed to do to make this dinner good enough for Jesus! Mary, on the other hand, just wanted to be with Jesus. She wanted to spend as much time with him as possible, so she sat at his feet, soaking up his every word.

Martha, distracted by everything that still needed to be done (and in true older sister fashion), fumed that Mary had left her with all the work. At one point, she even asked Jesus to tell Mary to help her! This is how Jesus responded: "Martha, Martha, you are worried and upset about many things, but few things are needed—or indeed only one. Mary has chosen what is better, and it will not be taken away from her" (Luke 10:41–42).

I'm guessing that was really hard for Martha to hear. She probably thought she was doing the right thing, making everything perfect for Jesus. But he pointed out that the most important thing was to sit at his feet and get to know him better. When the pressures of life build up, I try to remember that. Even if spending some time "sitting with Jesus" during my morning quiet time is the only thing I accomplish in a day, I've done something that will have lasting impact on me and those around me.

God doesn't call you to check off a list of good things. He calls you to an identity. He says, "You're mine, and everything you do should show that."

I love Micah 6:8, which lays out a simple plan for pleasing God. "And what does the Lord require of you? To act justly and to love mercy and to walk humbly with your God." As long as I'm seeking to love God better and to love those around me, I can have confidence that I'm doing what's right.

DARE (NOT) TO COMPARE

When I look at other people who are doing cool things, enjoying great relationships, or having major success, it can be tempting to compare myself to them or to want what they have. All of us have heroes in our lives and people we look up to, and that's okay. But we have to remember that each of us is created differently, and God has specific plans for each person.

God designed us to work together, and we each play a role. Some of those roles seem big while others seem small, but each is important. Comparing myself to others only steals my joy and causes me to miss out on what's going on in *my* life. When we accept the place where God has planted us, we can begin to bloom and spread joy.

I have a friend who works at Burger King and goes to a small community college. She'd be the first to admit that her life doesn't seem very glamorous. But she is incredibly happy all the time. People love to be around her because her joy is contagious. She is making a huge impact just by living faithfully where she is.

You may not love your current situation, but you can always love the people around you. And in the long run, that's what will make a lasting difference in the world and to those in your life.

DISCOVERING YOU

Maybe you feel like you have no idea who you are. People my age talk about needing to "find themselves" before they can do anything significant in this world. Discovering more about who you are and what makes

you tick can be a great thing. The problem comes when "finding myself" means chasing after the next thing that will entertain, interest me, or fill the void. That kind of searching quickly becomes focused only on me.

I recently heard this quote: "It's not about finding yourself, it's about discovering who God created you to be." I like that. As we get to know the one who created us, we can learn new things about ourselves and discover how he has made us different from every single other person in the world!

God gave each of us a unique set of passions, desires, and talents. It's okay to not know what you want to do with your life—you can trust that God will reveal those things to you. For example, I've realized that I have a passion for talking to people and giving them advice. I didn't

know that about myself until I started making advice videos for my YouTube channel. As I started sharing more of my heart, that passion started to grow.

Think about the things in your life that you enjoy. What are you talented at? What are you passionate about? Get involved in those things and watch how God uses you. He might even call you to do something that you don't think you're going to be great at . . . and you might nail it!

I definitely haven't lived a "normal" life since I started my YouTube channel. I've received some incredible opportunities and met some amazing people. This life hasn't always been easy or glamorous, but as I've followed God, I've been able to learn and grow even during the hard times.

My YouTube channel may not always have the success it has right now. Social media and technology are always changing. A few years from now, I could be doing something totally different. That's why I try to ask

FOUR WAYS TO DISCOVER THE TRUE YOU

You may not know exactly what God's calling you to do, or what your talents are, but here are a few simple things you can do to unearth your true identity:

1. **Look to God's Word.** One of the best ways you can discover who you are is to get to know the one who made you! Along with reading your Bible to find out all the things God says about you, try memorizing it. Choose a verse or passage to work on for a year or a month, write it down, and post it in a place where you'll see it often. Here are a few of my favorites for memorizing: Psalm 145:18–19, Proverbs 3:5–6, Romans 8:28, and Philippians 4:6–7.

2. **Focus on others.** Every day, look for ways to encourage and help the people around you. As you listen and spend time with those people, you will actually learn a lot about yourself.

3. **Do things for free.** Serve at your local church, babysit for a family who needs it, or do volunteer work in your community. If you're feeling really bold, go on a mission trip! Using your gifts to serve God and help others is a fulfilling way to discover how God has wired you.

4. **Try something new.** Have you ever heard the phrase, "You'll never know until you try"? Well, it's true. If you're struggling to find your identity, try out a new hobby or activity. Maybe you'll discover you love being on stage, have an aptitude for the clarinet, or are great at soccer. It's never too late to try something new. You might love it!

myself, "Where am I finding my identity and security?" Is it in the temporary success of popularity on social media? Or is it in the things that matter most—my family, my friends, and my faith?

I'm constantly reminded that life is short. You and I don't know how many days we have on this earth. Right now, you may be in an amazing time of your life where everything seems to be going your way and success comes easily. Or maybe it's the opposite: nothing is going right and you wonder why you're even here. Either way, your life has purpose, friend! Success is fleeting, and nobody experiences it all the time. But you can never know the impact you're having on the people around you, even in small, ordinary ways.

When I start to forget who I am, I remind myself that today I have the opportunity to serve God and make a difference in someone's life—even if it's just one person. A few years from now, my YouTube career may be in the past, but I know I'll be somewhere and doing something that is right for that time. My position or popularity may change, but my value never will. That's what it means to embrace my own beautiful—to be exactly the person I was created to be.

XOXO,

Chels

Insider Style Tip:

SIMPLE BEAUTY TRICKS FOR REAL WOMEN

Let's face it: we can't look ultra glamorous *every* day. But there are some easy tricks for achieving natural, everyday beauty. Here are some simple fixes for common beauty issues.

- **To soothe irritated skin:** After you wash your face, soak a washcloth in hot water, wring it out, and place it over your face until it's cold. This will open up your pores and allow your moisturizer to soak in more effectively. For dry skin, be sure to use a moisturizer without SPF or acne-fighting ingredients.
- **To cover blemishes:** Apply moisturizer to a clean face and wait a few minutes. Use regular foundation first and blend. Then use color-correcting concealer and blend until any remaining redness or blemishes disappear.
- **To give skin a natural glow:** Use an illuminating primer. Then apply makeup, and use a dewy finish setting spray to achieve additional glow.
- **To avoid looking tired:** Dab a red-tinted concealer (even bright red-orange lipstick works!) under your eyes. It may sound weird, but red will counteract the greenish-purple bags under your eyes that make you look tired.

- **To create fuller lashes:** Start by using a fine-tipped mascara, then apply a curved-tip mascara on top of that.
- **To look good after working out:** Use waterproof mascara during your workout. Afterward, blotting tissues are a lifesaver!
- **To create effortless waves:** My go-to method for creating pretty waves is to braid my hair the night before.

CHAPTER 12

LOOKING TO THE FUTURE

There is no need to fear the future, God is already there.

—ELISABETH ELLIOT

About a year ago, I had this sense that things were about to change. Have you ever felt that way? It seemed like an invisible wind was blowing through my life and stirring everything up.

What made that wind harder to manage was the fact I hadn't felt it coming. Four years earlier, my social media was taking off, thousands of people were watching and commenting on my videos, and I had confidence that big things were ahead. And somewhere in there, God also got ahold of my heart, fueling a passion to share my faith with others. Posting more faith videos, mixed in with my beauty and lifestyle posts, made me feel like I was making a real difference, and building something important.

When I graduated high school, I figured the next logical step in my journey was to head to an out-of-state college I loved and study communications and entrepreneurship. But leaving college after two weeks completely changed the future I had planned for myself. I often wondered what my future would look like, but all of those years I'd spent getting to know God gave me a quiet confidence that he was up to something. I sensed I just needed to wait. And wait I did.

I continued producing content for my channel, took up running, and settled back into quiet, small town life in Illinois. I plugged back into my church. I reconnected with the few friends who were still in the area. I was making a lot of videos centered on processing my journey of leaving college and depending on God, and I saw that those videos weren't getting as many views as some of my others.

At first that seemed like a bad thing, and I was feeling a little discouraged. But then I met with some Instagram representatives who keep an eye on influencers and monitor their overall social media statistics. They told me that my third-highest number of subscribers live in a city where few people are Christians. In fact, people there can be killed for being public about their faith in Christ. And we're not talking a couple hundred followers in that city, but thousands of people who watch my channel and pay attention to my content.

The reps also told me that my content was unique, since I am one of a few YouTubers sharing my faith in this format. I was thankful for their encouragement, but reminded them that my faith content didn't seem to be as popular with my followers. They assured me that I shouldn't give up on the path I was pursuing. Then they said, "You should come up with an idea to make this grow."

That suggestion stuck with me, but what could I do?

A NEW PASSION

Around the time I was thinking through what was next for me and my platform, I received an invitation to be a social media influencer for the Passion conference, which takes place every January. This is a Christian conference for college students, where thousands of young people gather every year to worship God together and hear amazing speakers.

FOUR WAYS TO MAKE DECISIONS FOR THE FUTURE

As you look to your future, it can be confusing to decide what to do. For instance, should you take a big plunge by moving away, or pursue an educational or career opportunity? Here are some steps that have helped me evaluate my options and make solid decisions:

Make a pros and cons list. As you already know, I love making lists! So when I have a big decision to make, I write down the pros and cons of making a certain choice. For example, if I'm trying to decide whether to move out of state, a pro would be "new opportunities and friends," while a con would be "losing the daily support of my family." On the reverse side of the paper, I make a separate list of pros and cons for the opposite choice. Thinking through the advantages and challenges of each option allows me to make an informed decision.

Ask someone older and wiser. A great way to gain valuable perspective on an important life decision is to talk to someone who has experienced a little more life than you. This could be a parent, a mentor, or an older friend. Proverbs 13:20 says, "Walk with the wise and become wise." When it comes to making decisions for the future, seek out all the wisdom you can find.

Remember the basics. Sometimes we agonize over decisions that should be simple to make. God calls all of us to live in certain ways. For example, we are all called to love other people and obey the instructions for living in God's Word. When I'm making a decision, I can first decide if it lines up with what the Bible says. If not, it's an easy no. But if the decision does line up, I can feel free to move forward.

Pray specifically. There have been a few times when I was really unsure about what decision I should make, so I prayed for specific confirmation in one direction or another. Philippians 4:6 says, "Do not be anxious about anything, but in every situation, by prayer and petition, with thanksgiving, present your requests to God." God wants to respond to your prayers! He answers in three ways: yes, no, or wait.

A few months before the conference, I did a Google hangout with the other members of the social media team. They were young people from around the country who had founded ministries, written books, and actively served in their churches. Like me, they had a significant presence on social media. And as we got to know each other better, we discovered that each of us have a heart for creating a revival among our generation through the massive reach of social media. We began using Ephesians 3:20 as a theme verse in our conversations, which says, "Now to him who is able to do immeasurably more than all we ask or imagine, according to his power that is at work within us, to him be glory in the church and in Christ Jesus throughout all generations, for ever and ever! Amen."

When I thought more about that verse, and how it inspired me, I suddenly realized God had something greater on the horizon.

That sense grew exponentially once I arrived at the Passion Conference itself. I joined more than 50,000 other eighteen- to-twenty-five-year-old Christians at the Georgia Dome in Atlanta, all with a shared purpose to not only worship God, but to discover ways our generation can use our lives and talents for things that matter.

There were big names there, such as Hillsong United, Carrie Underwood, and Francis Chan. But what impacted me the most was the

enthusiasm to see change and revival during our lifetimes. The second night I tweeted: "Fifty-five thousand people lifting up our Savior, Father & Redeemer. The power of the presence of the ONLY living God was so prevalent it's unexplainable."

In between speakers, I met with a group of eight strangers (who are now friends) to talk about what God was saying to us through the conference. While every speaker left me inspired, one thing I'd prayed about before attending Passion was that I'd develop more confidence in Christ. As I adjusted to the new path God had me on, I often struggled with a lot of questions and doubts.

One morning I almost missed my community group, but decided to go anyway and be late. When I arrived, the question on the screen was, "What is something that gives you confidence in God?" I knew I was supposed to be there.

During that session and throughout my time at Passion, I began to realize that I'm not alone. I'm not the only one who wants to make a difference in my generation and help people understand all that God has for them. I witnessed over 50,000 people who wanted to do something. Not in the future, but right now in the present.

One evidence of that was when conference attendees made history by sponsoring seven thousand children through Compassion International. It showed me again that my generation longs to make a positive change in our world—something we realize will only happen as we pursue the one who has the power to truly and permanently change hearts and lives.

But my biggest moment may have been the final night of the conference, when Passion founder Louie Giglio presented a powerful closing message. As I stood on the main floor with a few of the friends I'd met through social media months before, I was astonished while he preached on the passage we had been discussing before the conference, Ephesians 3:20–21.

I don't think God could have delivered any clearer confirmation to me and my friends that we were on the right track when it came to our social media platforms. In less than four months, God had totally changed my mindset and begun to reveal a new future more beautiful than the one I'd imagined. I was filled with profound gratitude and expectancy for what he would do next.

DITCHING WORRY

Right about now you may be thinking, *That's great for you, Chels. But what if I have no idea what I'm supposed to do next?*

I get it. Sometimes not knowing the future can drive you crazy. Maybe, like me, you've asked some of these questions:

- What will I do with my life?
- Who will I date or marry?
- Will I get into a good college?
- How will I make money?
- Will I have a family?

We all want to believe that we're destined for a great future with fulfilling work, great families, and the perfect home of our own. But, let's face it: there can be big obstacles in the way of achieving these goals. So thinking about the future is scary at times.

In Matthew 6:34, Jesus gave this very good reminder: "Therefore do not worry about tomorrow, for tomorrow will worry about itself. Each day has enough trouble of its own."

Isn't that the truth? When I look at the world around me, I can find plenty of things to worry about. Will everyone I love stay safe and healthy? Will I be able to provide for myself? Will I find love? Will I continue to grow my channel and my business? I once heard someone say that worry is like a rocking chair; it gives you something to do but gets you nowhere. Worrying about the future steals energy and brain space you could be using to enjoy today!

Of course, there are times when we can't help being concerned about things going on in our lives. And having suffered from anxiety, I understand worry well. But giving worry first place in my life can also put distance between me and God, because when I choose to worry, I may believe that God isn't in control or that he doesn't have my best interest in mind.

I figured out a long time ago that worrying about my future was a waste of time. So how do you get out of the worry trap? Here are a few things that have worked for me:

Focus on the present. When I'm feeling stressed about what the future might look like, I make a mental list of all of the things I'm thankful for today: Family. Health. Friends. Puppies. Seriously, today is full of evidence of God's goodness! Why would I doubt that he has anything less for me tomorrow? Or five years from now?

Practice dependence. We live in a very independent world, where we don't like to have to depend on others, let alone God, for what we need. But when worries about the future crop up, we're forced to trust that God has a plan. When my college plans got put on indefinite hold, I clung to Matthew 6:34, knowing that God's plans were still good.

Write it down. Making a list of worries or journaling about them can be a great stress reliever. The hand is slower than the mind, so writing out your thoughts slows them down and gives you time to gain some perspective. I like to write my worries in a journal, sometimes in the form of prayers, and then give them over to God.

However you choose to set aside worry, do it! Studies have found that as much as 85 percent of the things we worry about never happen. Dwelling on things that could go wrong in the future won't change anything; it will only make you less engaged in what great things are happening in your life today. Don't let worry about the future steal your present purpose and joy!

THE FUTURE IS NOW

Figuring out what you are supposed to do with your life isn't easy. When I took that 1,800-mile road trip to California, I was certain I was supposed to go to college, learn more about communications, and meet a few college BFFs! Boy, was I wrong.

Proverbs 16:9 has encouraged me when I'm feeling uncertain about the future. It says, "In their hearts humans plan their course, but the Lord establishes their steps." I may have a super-great plan for how my life is going to go, but in the end, God determines the path.

Back when my YouTube channel first started getting popular, I began to imagine a future for myself that involved makeup and fashion. I thought I might pursue a career in the beauty industry and possibly do makeup for the stars! But as my YouTube channel grew, I also discovered a passion for giving people advice that went beyond "How to Look Great for Date Night."

I've had a few moments where I felt pretty sure of what I would do with my life, but the moments where I've been unsure greatly outnumber them. Uncertainty is part of life. At times, it can make life really exciting—like when you wonder if a guy has feelings for you or if you're going to get that great internship or job you applied for.

Other times, uncertainty about what's going to happen can cause stress and even paralyze us from doing something or anything. One benefit of being a Christian, however, is that no matter how few details I know about the next week or year, there are some things I can know and act upon with certainty. Here are a few of them:

> **I am here for a reason.** Everything in God's creation has a
> specific purpose and reason for existing. No matter what I'm going
> through, or how uncertain my future is, God has the final result all
> mapped out. He created me with all of my specific strengths and
> weaknesses, equipping me to do things only I can do. Ephesians
> 2:10 says, "For we are God's handiwork, created in Christ Jesus

to do good works, which God prepared in advance for us to do." The fact God designed a specific "itinerary" for me and my life is exciting!

My main purpose in life is to love God and others. When Jesus was on earth, someone asked him what the greatest commandment was. His answer was surprisingly simple: "Love the Lord your God with all your heart and with all your soul and with all your mind . . . [and] love your neighbor as yourself" (Matthew 22:37, 39). I think we can all agree that our world needs more love. That's one of the reasons I'm so on board with Jesus. Whether I'm living at home, attending college, working, or pursuing a dream, I can love God and the people around me. My purpose doesn't need to be to change the world, but rather to love one person at a time as God brings them into my life.

God's instructions offer protection and safety. We can get uncomfortable talking about how God wants us to live and the things he wants us to avoid, because it feels so restrictive. It's way easier to do what you want and make all of your own decisions rather than to worry about what God wants you to do.

At times I've lived my own way, and it never led to anything good. I've learned the hard way that my own ideas aren't always best. When I'm faced with a decision about my future that involves doing something the Bible says is wrong, I can know right away it's not what God has for me.

I can trust God. This is a lesson I'm still learning. I often want to take back control of my life and know what the future holds. In those moments, I try to remember who holds the future and that he is completely trustworthy. Maybe people in your life have broken your trust, so it's hard for you to imagine someone who won't let you down. It may even seem too incredible to be true! But God's character can be trusted; he always tells the truth, is loving and good, and never changes. That is someone I can depend upon to have good plans for my life.

While there have been many times where the details of the future have been unclear, knowing how to live each day is pretty obvious. While I was reeling after leaving college, I depended on these basic truths about who I am and who God is until I could see the next step. Some days were really hard. It felt like walking through a thick fog, where I couldn't see anything around me, let alone what was ahead. But eventually the fog lifted so I could see that he'd laid the most wonderful path before me!

When I was obsessing over where I'd be in the next few years, I wasn't able to concentrate as fully on what God had for me in the moment. In every season, even the hard ones, there are opportunities to grow and learn things that will help us later on. If you find yourself feeling "stuck" and wondering if you even have a future, I'm here to tell you that you do! Hope and a future are things God offers freely. You never need to wonder if his plans are good.

Because of that, we don't have to fear the future. We can walk confidently in the opportunities God provides, one step at a time.

CHELSEA'S BUCKET LIST

I don't know everything my future holds, but I do have some dreams. Here are ten things I hope to do at some point in my life:

1. Visit another country.
2. Swim with dolphins.
3. Learn how to ice skate backward.
4. Read at least twenty-five books every year.
5. Go skydiving.
6. Get really good at a musical instrument.
7. Adopt a child.
8. Decorate my own home.
9. Bring the Word of God to as many places as possible.
10. Learn how to longboard like a pro.

THE FUTURE IS BRIGHT

When I first began writing this book, I assumed that in this chapter I would be telling you all about college and my future career goals. Instead, I've been honored to share how God "broke me" and made me into something brand new.

In Japan, they practice an art called Kintsugi, where the artist repairs broken pottery by filling the cracks with gold or silver. This makes the piece even more beautiful than it was to begin with and honors the breaking and the repair as a beautiful part of the object's history, rather than something to hide.

I believe God has done something similar in my life. And I don't regret a single crack, because he has made my life more beautiful than

before. Every up and down has strengthened me and shaped my character to prepare me for this very moment.

My life has radically changed since I stood on that stage at the NYX Face Awards as a wide-eyed fourteen-year-old with big dreams of making a splash on YouTube. At times I have to laugh at how clueless I was. But God knew all along what BeautyLiciousInsider would turn out to be.

I have no plans to leave behind my makeup and beauty roots. Sharing outfits of the day and helping women feel good about how they look remains a passion of mine. I believe it's only when we realize how beautiful we are, exactly the way God created us, that we can reflect real beauty to the world. But I've also gained a greater vision for what I'm doing.

I want to inspire everyone who uses social media—especially my generation—to be a light to the world through this powerful medium. As I pursue the dreams God has given me, I hope to inspire others to pursue the dreams he's given them.

You, my friend, are a huge part of that! As you discover the ways in which God has made you one of a kind—find your own beautiful—you will be free to make a difference in this world in ways that only you can. I have no doubt that you will do great things.

And that's beautiful.

XOXO,

Chels

Insider Style Tip:

GROWING UP YOUR LOOK

Fashion and style are constantly changing. I've learned that my personal style needs to keep developing too. Whether you need a sophisticated look for a job interview or college classes, or you just want a more grown-up approach to fashion, here are some tips to step up your look:

Ditch the denim. A jean jacket can be a very cute choice, but swap it out for a faux-leather jacket to dress up any outfit. Also, give your favorite pair of jeans a break by wearing a different style of pants or even a skirt once a week.

Play with color. Neutral colors—such as navy, black, white, tan, and brown—can give you a polished, timeless look. If you love color (I do!), add a pop of your favorite hue with a cute bag, shoes, or eye shadow.

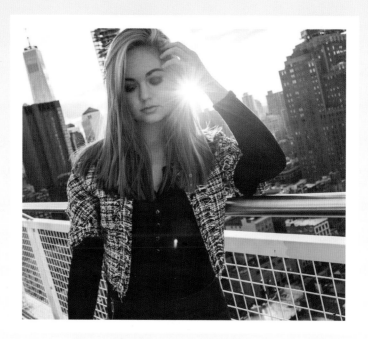

Tuck in your shirt. Not only does a tucked-in button-up shirt look neat and tidy, it also gives you the opportunity to showcase a fabulous belt! Build your outfit around a great belt that shapes your clothes to your body.

Choose structured pieces. An A-line dress or structured jacket adds immediate sophistication to your look. Thicker fabrics also create clean lines and make you appear more put together.

Accessorize intelligently. Wearing lots of accessories can be fun, fun, fun! But if you're off to a job interview or meeting where you need to make a great first impression, less is more. Choose one or two accents, such as a scarf or a beautiful pair of earrings, and allow the real you to shine through.

Dress it up. Sometimes I can go days without "dressing up." Choosing a simple touch, such as a pretty bracelet or cute shoes, can instantly take your look up a notch.

Remember to "switch up" your look often so you don't get stuck in a rut. New experiences provide a great opportunity to play with your style so that it's constantly evolving—just like you.

ACKNOWLEDGMENTS

I want to thank so many people for not only making this book happen, but for investing in Christ and pouring into this book with me.

Larry Shapiro—Thank you so much for believing in me. I know there have been many moments when you have wondered how I'd grow. You knew I'd grow; you just did not know how. I am inspired by you. Thank you for setting a great example of what a hardworking man looks like. You are the man to go to if I want to get something done! You are the best manager I have ever had.

Cassie Hanjian—Thank you for being so intentional with me and for making sure Christ was always portrayed on the page the way he is in the Bible. This is so important, and you know the weight of that. You have a gift for understanding the audience as well. Thank you so much for your astounding friendship and for being a God-given agent.

Suzanne Gosselin—I am overwhelmed with thankfulness for you. Thank you for being such an amazing example of what it's like to wait on the Lord. Thank you for holding my hand throughout this process and helping me find the right words to both show how God has worked in my life and give him the ultimate glory.

Emmie Seaton—Thank you so much for helping keep this book on track! I always love spending time with you and am so thankful for your friendship and wisdom. I know you are going to do amazing things for the Kingdom.

Thank you to my editor, Jillian Manning, for patiently and skillfully coaching me through the process of writing my first book.

Thank you to Sal Cincotta for using your amazing talent to make the photography for this book rock!

Special thanks also to Annette Bourland and Londa Alderink for believing in this project from the very beginning.

And thanks to the wonderful team at Zondervan—Ron Huizinga (cover design), Jacque Alberta (developmental editing), Denise Froehlich (interior design), Kim Tanner (photos and digital assets), Liane Worthington (PR manager), and Marcus Drenth (marketing manager)—for supporting this project through your excellent talents.

I also want to thank a few friends, new and old:

Louie Giglio—You handed off the baton to this chosen generation. Thank you for your obedience to the Lord.

Lysa TerKeurst—Your sweet and humble nature are two qualities I hope to gain in my walk with Christ. You are one of the most effective communicators out there, and I thank you for pouring your advice and wisdom into my life. I love you and your family with all my heart.

The Alternative—Thank you for giving the people of this world an alternative to the typical Saturday night. I pray that people will choose this event over walking into a bar or club. Jesus is greater, better, and wants more for us. He cares for us so much that he loves us where we are at, but he also wants to change us from the inside out.

Lee Strobel—You are incredible. Thank you for bestowing so much knowledge and wise council throughout the process of book promotion.

Ravi Zacharias—Thank you for living the life worthy of your calling and always being prepared to give an answer for the hope you have in Christ Jesus.

Matt Brown—Jesus always loved to form friendships with others, and that is what you do. Thank you for always being willing to share your resources for his glory!

To all of those with whom I attended high school—Thank you for supporting my YouTube channel. You saw the growth, but I am here to say it was all God. I miss you guys and pray God is doing abundantly more than you ever ask or imagine for the Kingdom through you.

Charis and Jacob—Charis, I cannot begin to put into words the significance of your influence in my life. Thank you for your contagious love for Jesus and willingness to chat or pray with me at any hour of the day or night. Jacob, thank you for being an example of a godly husband who loves his wife. The two of you are an awesome example of marriage and loving and following Jesus together—giving him all glory.

And my profound thanks to my family for supporting me throughout this process and throughout life.

Dad, you have pushed me to work hard and do my best since I was a little girl. You have always wanted good things for me. You are a true example of what Christ looks like in a godly man.

Mom, thanks for being weird, strange, and all together lovely. We were born in two different generations, but God has made us similar in so many ways. I look up to you as a model for how I will nurture and love my kids someday. I love you. Thank you for being there for me through depression. You let Christ lead you and therefore were my rock in that circumstance.

Chandler, you make me laugh every day. You are going to make your future wife laugh uncontrollably. I cannot wait to see you share the gospel through comedy.

Kylie, I know you have been through a lot. I love you so much, and so does our Heavenly Father. I cannot wait to see the ways God uses you to bring healing to people through science and medicine. You are so intelligent and driven, and I see a lot of our dad in you. Your work ethic inspires me, and I love you.

And most of all, thanks to my Lord and Savior, Jesus Christ, who no longer lets me live in shame, doubt, fear, pain, guilt, disobedience, rebellion, lust, addiction, depression, or disease. I thank him for always having open arms when we screw up. I thank him for being faithful through the mess and carrying us up the mountain so we can embrace him at the top. Although we are free, we must take action in the gospel and live in that freedom. I am free in his name. In his name the darkness is exposed with light, the prisoners take refuge in him, the sheep flock to the shepherd, the blind can now see, the fatherless are adopted into a family, the lame can now walk, the mute can now speak, the broken-hearted are bound in love, and the world is in his hands. My heart longs for more of you, Jesus. I can't wait until my soul dances in your presence.

Chelsea Crockett made her debut on YouTube as Beauty-LiciousInsider in 2011, and has since gone on to become a role model for millions of teens around the globe. Her channel features makeup tutorials, life advice videos, and everything in between, including messages about Chelsea's faith. Chelsea has appeared in *Seventeen*, *Teen Vogue*, and *Trend Magazine*, among others, and her website, ChelseaCrockett.com, is home to thousands of beauty, fashion, lifestyle, and advice posts. Chelsea's greatest passion is connecting with her fans and subscribers and using her voice to make a positive impact on viewers across the world.